THE CHURCH

RICK BUNDSCHUH

Regal Books
A Division of GL Publications
Ventura, California, U.S.A.

Published by Regal Books
A Division of GL Publications
Ventura, California 93006
Printed in U.S.A.

The authors and publisher have sought to locate and secure permission to reprint copyrighted materials in this book. If any such acknowledgments have been omitted, the publisher would appreciate receiving the information so that proper credit may be given in future printings.

Scripture quotations in this book are taken from the *HOLY BIBLE: NEW INTERNATIONAL VERSION*. Copyright © 1973, 1978, 1984 by the International Bible Society. Used by permission of Zondervan Bible Publishers.

© Copyright 1988 by Regal Books
All rights reserved.

Library of Congress Cataloging-in-Publication Data

Bundschuh, Rick, 1951-
   The church / by Rick Bundschuh.
     p.   cm.
   Includes bibliographies.
   ISBN 0-8307-1182-1
   1. Bible. N.T. Timothy, 1st—Criticism, interpretation, etc. 2. Church—Biblical teaching. I. Tit.e
BS2745.2.B86   1988
262—dc19   88-9692
                                                                              CIP

2 3 4 5 6 7 8 9 10/ 92 91 90 89

Rights for publishing this book in other languages are contracted by Gospel Literature International (GLINT) foundation. GLINT also provides technical help for the adaptation, translation, and publishing of Bible study resources and books in scores of languages worldwide. For further information, contact GLINT, Post Office Box 488, Rosemead, California, 91770, U.S.A., or the publisher.

CONTENTS

Preface   7

1   This Is the Church, This Is the Steeple . . .   9
Knowing something about the sometimes surprising history of the Church helps Christians get a perspective on some church practices.

2   More than Warming a Pew   21
The real Church is made up of real Christians.

3   Avoiding Infections   33
To stay spiritually well Christians must avoid being infected by worldliness and sin.

4   The Gilded Trap   45
Affluence can be dangerous.

5   The Shepherd   55
The Bible lists qualifications and guidelines for Church leaders.

6   Women in the Church   67
Christians must separate cultural bias from biblical guidelines when determining what roles women can have in the Church.

7 Don't Look Down on Youth 79
Young people are a vital part of the Church.

8 Rotten Apples in the Barrel 91
Christians must be firmly grounded in the Word in order to recognize false teachers.

9 Shipwrecked Faith 103
Ignoring the guidance of conscience can have a disastrous effect on faith.

10 The Church and the "Least of These" 115
Pure service to the Lord means caring for needy, often-overlooked people.

11 God Has No Favorites—
the Church Shouldn't Either 127
All people should matter to Christians.

12 The Heartbeat of God 139
Worship and prayer connect Christians with God.

*To Dick and Dottie Anderson
who showed me a church where
Christ was in charge.*

PREFACE

Most of the ideas that will be presented in this book are based on themes found in a very short but interesting part of the New Testament—1 Timothy. First Timothy is really a personal letter written around A.D. 65 and sent from the apostle Paul to his young friend and former traveling companion, Timothy. So, in a sense we are really opening someone else's mail when we read this letter. I think God intended for us to do this. It is certain that Timothy shared his mail with others. Timothy's letter from Paul was copied and dispersed throughout various first-century churches. The sharing of apostles' letters was one of the ways early church leaders encouraged other believers. First Timothy has continued being one of the tools that God has used to inspire and urge on Christians through the ages.

This letter is really all about the Church. Although it was written specifically to Timothy who was a leader in the church at Ephesus, it deals in many places with the ideas that any group of Christians should live by.

Naturally there are many things about the way Christian people should live and behave that are not found in this letter. Therefore, I have tried to include issues that are suggested by the ideas Paul wrote in 1 Timothy. I have tried to expand some of the information by using other compatible teachings from the Bible.

Timothy was probably an apostolic representative to the believers in a city called Ephesus. Tradition says that he continued to work with the Christians at Ephesus until

8 THE CHURCH

he was killed by order of the Roman Emperor.

But even the power of Rome could not stop the earth-shaking Church. Within a few hundred years the shaking would topple the paganism of imperial Rome and its emperor would declare himself among the earth shakers!

ONE

THIS IS THE CHURCH, THIS IS THE STEEPLE...

*I am writing you these instructions so that
. . . you will know how people ought to conduct themselves in God's household, which is the church of the living God.*
1 Timothy 3:14,15

Picture yourself weaving down a narrow alleyway. The street is made of cobblestone. It sinks noticeably in the places where the constant friction of cart wheels have worn grooves. The walls of the buildings are stucco. Most carry a montage of messages urging you to buy slaves at the marketplace this Wednesday or to attend the fights at the amphitheater. Some of the messages are crude graffiti hurling insults at a noble family. Others are simply random carvings of a name—"Apollo was here"—a simple way to insure that something of the writer will be left on this earth.

One thing that strikes you as strange (since you are from out of town) are the smells and the noises of the district. There are aromas that you have never smelled before—some kind of food cooking that you have never tasted. The pungent smell of sweat and raw sewage mixed with the fragrance of bittersweet spices wafts through the air.

The narrow alleyway is packed with people and the houses are not only built closely to each other but many of them are also stacked up three or four stories high. Whole families may live in 8 × 8-foot cubicles. It's easy to see this is definitely not the nicest part of the city.

Your guide suddenly ducks into a narrow doorway and leads you into a room dimly lit by four smoldering oil lamps. The room is full of people. A vast array of faces turn to greet you. Some of these people are old and toothless, some are poorly clad, many are foreign (like yourself), some are bearded and wear head coverings, others are clean shaven and are slaves.

Welcome to the Church.

You will find no pews here. You will not have a hymnal nor see an organ, stained glass, offering plate, pulpit, ushers, greeters, or any of the other things that might remind you of a church that you have previously known.

The people are crowded into a home of one of the believers (the Church will not have a single church building for nearly two hundred years)[1]. They are preparing to celebrate the Lord's Supper, but they seem to have enough food to feed an army. Actually they are planning to have a whole meal together.[2] This celebration will only vaguely remind you of Communion as it is served in most of the churches you've attended. These Christians have never heard of Sunday School, youth camp, or TV evangelists. Yet they are just as much the Church as the people in your hometown church. As a matter of fact, they are often held as an example of pure Christianity.

The people in this room are just a small number of the believers in the city you are visiting (which you discover to be Ephesus). There are dozens of similar meetings taking place all over the city. The people have not announced their meetings in the local paper nor have they placed glowing crosses outside of the homes in which they meet. But they are not particularly secretive. The meeting is kind of like a private party for those who are already initiated into the faith practiced by Christ's followers.

You have just stepped back to A.D. 65. You have witnessed what for the next several hundred years will be referred to as the "Church." It is the same kind of church that the apostles would address in many letters (many of which would find their way into the book we call the Bible). It is a church that is in many ways very, very different from ours. Yet in some ways it is very similar.

If we use the word the way it is used in the Bible, the Church is never a building. Rather the Church is people who believe in Jesus Christ as Savior and Lord. The child's finger game, "This is the church, this is the steeple, open the doors and see all the people" is absolutely incorrect from the Bible's point of view.

A Church pure and simple is believing people. (The word "church" as it is used in the New Testament is often translated from a Greek word meaning "assembly.") A small group of believers is all that is needed to qualify as a church. Yet when modern Christians think of the Church we almost automatically picture it as a building with all of the traditional religious trappings: pews, altars, hymnals, perhaps religious art. We also almost always think of a name: First Church, Elm Street Church, Community Church. Or we think of a denomination: the Catholic Church, the Baptist Church, the Foursquare Church.

It seems that what a Church really is has gotten a bit confused over the years. Where did all the buildings, fixtures, and names come from? Are they good for true Christianity or are they extra baggage that has somehow gotten dragged along with it?

If these questions were not enough there is even a confusing use of the word "church" in the Bible. Sometimes when the word is used it means the universal

Church, or in other words, all of the Christians everywhere no matter what city they live in or who leads them.[3] (the word *catholic* means "universal." It's original use implied that there were no significant divisions in the Church. It has come to mean a denomination that developed out of the church at Rome.)

You can see examples of this kind of "everybody everywhere who is a Christian" use of the word "church" by looking at the way Paul addressed one of his letters to the Corinthians: "To the church of God in Corinth, together with all the saints throughout Achaia."[4]

There is also another way the word "church" is used. It can call attention to a specific group of believers, for example: "the church at Jerusalem"[5] or "the church that meets at their house."[6] This could mean all the Christians in one particular city or all of the Christians who happen to meet at one house in one particular city.

What really adds confusion to the matter is our mixed up idea of what a church is. History has not helped to clarify the idea of what a church is supposed to be either. Somehow people have gotten the idea that the Church is a building or organization.

Originally the Church was under the leadership of the apostles. For awhile that leadership was located in Jerusalem until around A.D. 70 when Jerusalem was destroyed by the Romans. The Jerusalem Church scattered, important centers of Christianity sprang up in Rome, Antioch, Constantinople, Alexandria, and other cities. The leaders in each of these centers operated independently, but generally Christians still considered themselves to be members of the same body. (Eventually only the leadership in Rome and Constantinople had any significant power or authority.)

14 THE CHURCH

Around the fourth century politics muddied the identity of the Church. In A.D. 313 after suffering periods of persecution since the death of Jesus, Christians were granted the liberty to follow their faith by the Roman Emperor Constantine. Constantine became a Christian and suddenly Christianity was the "in" thing. Since Constantine favored Christians in every way, many of his subjects professed belief merely to gain his favor. These people who infiltrated the Church brought with them many practices from their pagan religions.

When the Emperor Theodosius (A.D. 378-398) made Christianity the state religion of the Roman Empire the "paganization" of the Church increased. The Imperial Church became very different from the persecuted early church of the first three centuries.[7] More and more the church became an organization with a hierarchy. The concept of all believers being important, equal members in a body that was Christ's representation on earth began to die.

The affairs of the government (as well as the social climbers) tangled up with the interests of a faith which had, until then, firmly renounced the world. Without a good background of biblical teaching and without an understanding of God as revealed in His dealings with the Jews, many new believers mixed their old pagan ways with their new faith. The simple worship of earlier Christians was developed into elaborate ceremonies. Church buildings and church services imitated the grand outward appearances of the pagan rituals and pagan temples. The image of the Church was made over from a group of equal, faithful people who were joined together by their common belief in Jesus as Lord to a group of people who were taking on the characteristics of Imperial Rome. Bishops of the various cities that were Christian centers had power not only over matters within the Church but also in politics. These bishops began to struggle over doctrinal issues and over who had the most authority.

When the Roman Empire split in A.D. 395, the Church began to separate into two distinct parts: the western church, centered in Rome and the eastern church, centered in Constantinople. The bishop of Rome tried to claim authority over all the Church but was largely disregarded until A.D. 590. In that year the bishop of Rome became the first real pope—Pope Gregory I.[8] Gregory worked very hard to purify the Church. He tried to rid the Church of many of the practices that had roots in paganism. And although he had no authority over the eastern church, he was greatly respected by its members.

But Gregory was unusual in his devotion. The central leadership of the church was rusting at its spiritual core. By A.D. 800 the leaders were living with mistresses, committing murder, starting wars, and basically acting like a bunch of outlaws. The first big church split occurred at this time. The eastern block of Christians formed their own, less corrupt church (now known as the Eastern or Greek Orthodox Church). The western or Roman Catholic Church was to go through more decay. But there were bright spots. Godly men such as Francis of Assisi (1181-1226), Thomas Aquinas (1225-1274), John Wycliffe (1324-1384), and John Huss (1369-1415) influenced people to re-examine their beliefs and church practice. But largely the Church lost its true identity. Personal Bible study was outlawed. Reading the Scriptures became the privilege of clergy. (Few people could read or were wealthy enough to own a Bible anyway.) Church offices could be bought. Popes and bishops became the richest men in Europe. By

1198 the pope was so powerful that he could overthrow kings who did not meet his approval.

This continued until 1508 when a monk named Martin Luther set off a spark which exploded the Church of Rome.

Luther never intended to break from the Roman Church, he merely wanted to point out some areas where the words of Scripture and the policy of the Roman church were at odds. He figured that the church administrators would see their error and change things. They didn't. In fact they became angry and ordered Martin Luther to recant (declare as false) his objections. Luther, astonished, refused. Martin got the boot from the priesthood and his followers became known as Lutherans. This was the first protestant church.[9] The name "protestant" comes from the idea that these Christians "protested" against the teachings of the Roman Church.

Since the time of Martin Luther many other groups have broken from their parent churches. They have fractured into so many brands of Christianity that it is hard to keep them straight. Some of these groups of believers were started by thoughtful people who were contemporaries of Luther. Other groups were started later. All these brands of Christianity are called "denominations." Often Christians of particular denominations think that their brand is the closest to the original formula for Christianity, is the best, or the most inspired. Some of those brands even say you aren't a Christian unless you belong to their particular kind of church.

Quite separate from denominations are cults. Cults are groups who fall so far from believing the things that all Christians, regardless of brand name, believe that they are not even in the ball park. Mormons and Jehovah's Wit-

THIS IS THE CHURCH, THIS IS THE STEEPLE... 17

nesses are two examples of these. Of course they think they have a new and improved message from God. But their teaching is definitely not biblical.

There are many things in Christianity that people have created to help people do a better job of worshiping God. For example, the division of Bible books into chapters and verses was a later development to help people find their way around in Scripture. These divisions were not in the original version but are so helpful that we have decided to keep them.[10] Stained glass windows were created to give the illiterate church members visual bits of Bible stories and to enhance the light of the dark churches of the Middle Ages. Light was revered and was associated with Jesus since He is "the light of men."[11] Church bells were used to call people to worship before there were clocks or watches. The bells were very practical—for awhile. Now many church bells are sort of outdoor amplified music boxes—pretty but not as practical. Some other things, like bells, were very effective for the times in which they were created but now have no real use. They have simply become part of the "tradition" of churches. Tradition means "things we have done for years and years and which will probably be around for awhile."

Other things that seem like they have been around for a long time are really relatively new. For example Sunday School was introduced during the industrial revolution as a means to educate poor children who worked in factories all week.[12] The aim was to improve both their physical and social conditions by education and to introduce them to Christianity by using the Bible as the main textbook and primer. This movement was considered evil by many churches of the day, but after a rocky start it was almost universally adopted.

Church pews used to be rented. The richer the family the closer to the front was their pew. Some popular churches had special pews in the back for the very poor. But often you had to wait in line to get a seat. This was the common way to raise the money to operate the church. Only on special occasions was the offering plate passed. The custom of renting pews only died out at the end of the last century.

Youth groups as we know them today were virtually unknown until after World War II. Few churches had a special person hired to work with kids (youth pastor) until the early 1970s.

Returning to the people we visited in the dim living room of an Ephesus home at the beginning of this chapter, consider the differences between the early church and church practice today. They didn't know anything about pews, steeples, pulpits, baptismals, youth groups, Christian rock, or altar calls. Yet, they were the Church just as much as we are. And their ministries were far more effective than the most sophisticated ministries of our day.

One thing is certain, the Christians of the early days could hardly afford to have a smug attitude towards the believers down the road or in the next town. In fact, they rejoiced at the arrival of any new Christian and made a great effort to make visitors or newcomers feel at home. There was little of the "my church is better than your church" or "my church is more spiritual than your church" attitudes found among them. Rather they were united by a hunger for news of the good things that God was doing in the neighbor church.

And when things got tough in one congregation, whether the distress was caused by famine, natural disaster, or war, the little house churches did not think twice about gathering up funds and rushing them to the aid of their fellow Christians.[13]

It is safe to say that if these early believers were suddenly transported into our culture they would be baffled and deeply saddened by the sight of groups of believers who would not cooperate with each other and who spent huge amounts of energy criticizing each other. Without use of TV, radio, or a printing press the early Christians managed to transform the world. You and I are the results of what God did through them. Maybe there is something we can learn from them. Maybe it is time to get back to basics.

DISCUSSION QUESTIONS

How has the content of this chapter influenced your understanding of what the Church is?

Looking at the events from church history, what basic beliefs and standards do you think the Church needs to maintain to be acceptable to God? At what point would you describe a group as non-Christian? (See 1 John 3:21—4:3 if you need help.)

When you are gathered with other members of the Church, what experiences do you find meaningful? Hard to understand?

NOTES
1. The first church building was erected during the reign of Alexander Severus (A.D. 222-235). (Henry H. Halley, *Halley's Bible Handbook* [Grand Rapids: Zondervan Publishing House, 1965], p. 760).

20 THE CHURCH

2. Romans 16:5
3. Matthew 16:18; 1 Timothy 3:5
4. 2 Corinthians 1:1
5. Acts 8:1
6. 1 Corinthians 16:19
7. *Halley's Bible Handbook*, pp. 759-760.
8. *Halley's Bible Handbook*, p. 771.
9. Baker, Robert A., *A Summary of Christian History* (Nashville: Broadman Press, 1959), p. 195.
10. Chapter and verse divisions were placed in the Bible by Cardinal Caro in 1236 and by Robert Stephens in 1551. (*Halley's Bible Handbook*, p.755).
11. John 1:4
12. The Sunday School movement was started by Robert Raikes in Gloucester, England, 1780.
13. Acts 11:27-30

TWO
MORE THAN WARMING A PEW

Fight the good fight of the faith. Take hold of the eternal life to which you were called. 1 Timothy 6:12

Being raised in a church does not make you a Christian any more than being born in an oven makes you a biscuit. But many people have the false idea that they will somehow absorb Christianity by putting in time on a pew.

The real Church is not a building, but a group of people who hold the same vital thing in common: a saving belief in Jesus Christ. Because we have confused the idea of what the genuine Church is, it is very possible to know people with the odd combination of Christian mannerisms and even speech, but who are not really true members of the biblical Church.

A number of years ago I was invited by an acquaintance to attend an unusual church. Many of us have been invited to church by friends. But what made this case unusual was the fact that the person who invited me was an avowed homosexual. The congregation of this unusual church was predominantly homosexual men and women. This man's motive for inviting me to a service was to prove that the homosexual community was as devoted to Christianity as the heterosexual community. I accepted the invitation, but decided to take along my girl friend so that there would be no misunderstandings.

As my girl friend and I arrived at the church building we were struck by the obvious attempt of many of the men and women to imitate the opposite sex by their dress and by their behavior. Many of the men affected effeminate lisps and moves. Many of the women were acting "butch." This group certainly made no secret of their homosexuality.

My acquaintance guided us to the second row of pews where we sang a few hymns (led by a talented but flaming "queen" on the organ). We were entertained by the all male choir, who very professionally sang a mellow pop song about love making the world go around. The offering was passed. (We declined to give our support that morning.) Then the preacher mounted the stage and delivered a warm fuzzy sermon about loving each other. As he spoke I could tell that the meaning he twisted from the verses he used that morning was very different from what the inspired writers of the Bible had in mind.

After the sermon an elder got up and closed the service by urging the congregation to greet each other with a "holy kiss." In fact, there were several men in the rear near the exit who were quite ready to provide this "service of ministry." (They kissed each member who passed by, much like a preacher stands at the rear of the church to shake the hands of exiting worshipers.) My girl friend and I made our escape through a side door.

Needless to say, this "church" had imitated, sometimes with better outward quality, all of the ritual used in the average church service. But whether these avowed and practicing gay men and women really qualify as members of the biblical Church is very questionable. Something is missing. In this case what's missing is obedience to the clear teaching of Scripture about sexual behavior.[1]

But something can be missing even in the midst of Scripture.

Jennifer had been raised in a Christian family. She had been going to the church building on the corner of Main and Ash streets for as long as she could remember.

Stored permanently somewhere in her mind were innumerable Bible verses drilled into her by Sunday School teachers. She also had a basic knowledge of the Old and New Testaments, particularly the stories and parables. Along with this pious material Jennifer also knew an assorted collection of facts having to do with how many books were in the Bible, their names, and locations.

But all of this good information could not keep Jennifer from changing, and she was not changing for the better. Inside of her whirled a tornado of anger, resentment, bitterness, pessimism, and rebellion. The change was not yet obvious on the outside, but it would start erupting in time.

Jennifer sat in the pew, went to youth group, sang Christian songs, and walked through the paces of being a "good little Christian girl." But inside she wanted nothing to do with the Church. She went to church activities only to insure an easy time doing what she really wanted to do, which was to break away and live in the fast lane for awhile. Jennifer cared little for God and His will for her. She wanted to try life *her* way, to make her own choices and to decide what was right for herself rather than be dictated to by ANYONE, whether it be parents, teachers, ministers, or God.

Jennifer knew that she was just a few short steps away from living the same double life on the outside that she was already living inside. She already had decided that if she could get Josh Randell as her boyfriend she would give him any sexual favor he wanted. And it was only a matter of time and circumstances when she would find the opportunity to get "loaded out of her mind." The only thing that held her actions in check was her fear of getting caught by her parents. Sitting in church each Sunday was the perfect smoke screen. Even if her parents had suspicions, her smiling, angelic face and sweetly singing voice would be sure to dissolve their fears. She would play the church game as long as she could work it to her advantage.

Jennifer was not a part of the Church even though she went faithfully each week and sang hymns with fervor. She was a play actor; she was a hypocrite.

There are many Jennifers warming pews all around the nation. Some of them are trying desperately to "serve two masters," something that Jesus said could not be done.[2] Some are coming for their weekly cleansing so they can go out and get messed up again. They do not wish to change but merely try to scrape some of the guilt off their souls.

What was missing for Jennifer was the vital element that transforms a person into a member of the true Church—a personal relationship with Jesus Christ. Jennifer could not have that relationship because she did not want it. Her choices would finally take her a long, long way from the vital element and ultimately from the Church itself.

No one is a Christian merely because his or her parents are. Christianity is not genetic. A good understanding of Christianity can be provided in the home, but parents cannot make the choice of obedience to God for their child. God doesn't have any grandchildren.

A person does not evolve into a Christian. It is a step, a line that one must cross and a specific choice that one must make. It is true that many people draw closer and closer to Christianity before making a commitment of their lives to it. Not all conversions are dramatic rescues from the gutter of life. But there comes a point, even if we cannot remember exactly when it was, that we put up the white flag and surrendered our will to God. Often this drawing closer to becoming a Christian has much to do with the company we are keeping or a particular person who influences us towards believing in Christ. But it is a mistake to think that we are Christians because we hang out with Christians. We may see better in the dark because of our proximity to the light but that does not mean that we have light within us.

Christianity is not a club. You do not join it for sport or because your relatives all belong. You do not have to pass initiation rites or perform mighty feats of valor. Accepting Jesus, becoming a member of God's family and therefore the Church is a very personal and private decision.

But there are common connections between all Christians. The central belief held by all truly Christian churches is the belief that God came to earth as a man who was tempted just like we are, who felt the pain of rejection, and who though innocent was cruelly put to death like a common criminal. This God/man told people that He was the One promised in all the Old Testament writings about the Messiah. He claimed the power to forgive sins and to grant everlasting life. He proved those claims to be fact while He walked the earth, by His miracles and by His resurrection.

Christians believe that through the sacrificial death of this innocent God/man they are able to be set free from their old selfish way of thinking and acting and are able to become more like God Himself. They believe that becoming a member of the *real* Church makes each person equal with others regardless of race, status, sex, background, or economics. Christians believe that through Jesus Christ they have become brothers and sisters who have the same heavenly Father. They also believe that by being a member of this Church they can help each other grow and develop in ways that were not possible before. But Christians also believe that there is only one way to become a true member of this group of people called the Church. A person becomes a member of the Church by putting his or her faith in Christ as Lord and Savior. Or to put it another way, people must choose to have God be their boss. Christians must try to find out what Jesus wants them to do and then do it, even if it is hard to go against what they would really prefer to do at the time (and it often will).

This does not mean that a member of God's Church is perfect. No way! We are more like small children who will try to get away with as much as we can. Christians can even be down right disobedient at times. But we still know who our Father is and will ultimately obey Him.

Becoming a Christian does not depend on being good enough to impress God. He is not impressed. Becoming a Christian is not connected with putting on a performance for God. Crawling miles on our knees or going to church services every time the doors are open will make us no more attractive to God. He loves us just like we are. He wants us just like we are, but He will not let us stay that way. Perhaps the following illustration will help to explain my point.

Once upon a time there were two young brothers. One loved to roll in the dirt, slide down hills, crawl on the roof, and basically do anything he could to get filthy. The other brother was far more quiet. He enjoyed coloring and drawing more than outdoor activities.

One day the boys' father announced that the entire family would be going to visit relatives. In preparation, the boys were to get a thorough scrubbing. The active boy, although he was at the stage in life where he didn't like water, could see that a bath was in order. He was given a sound scouring with a brush and plenty of soap and shampoo. For the time being he was spotlessly clean.

When the boys' father announced to the quiet son that it was his bath time, the young boy squealed in protest. From the boy's point of view he was not dirty or in need of a bath. But the father saw things differently and gave the boy the exact same kind of scrubbing that he had given the more visibly dirty son. In the end they both got a thorough washing.

This is how it is with God and us. He doesn't want us to clean up for Him, He will do that for us. We can't impress Him with how clean we are, we will get scrubbed anyhow.

The Bible puts it this way: "For it is by grace you have been saved, through faith—and this not from yourselves, it is the gift of God—not by works, so that no one can boast."[3]

Even though faith in Christ is what makes a person a member of God's Church, a Christian, many bodies of believers require things in order to become a voting member of their group. Sometimes their requirements have to do with a particular belief they emphasize, sometimes it is for a more practical reason such as to screen out those who want to join the Church for the wrong reasons.

Ironically, it is possible to join a church organization, contribute, actively participate, and look pious to everyone around and still not really be a member of the true "Church."

But a word of caution here is very important. Christians are not the final judges of who is a valid member of God's family. God is the judge. True Christianity has little to do with the manner of worship that people use to enjoy God, whether they hold their hands up or put them down when they sing, whether they repeat prayers from an old prayer book, or whether they fall flat on their face. It also may have little to do with being right on every doctrine or subject in the Bible. Jesus never said you have to be correct in all of your ideas about theology to get to heaven. He did say you have to believe in Him.

Believing in Christ is not a whimsical thing that we do. It is not a walk in the park, a warm fuzzy, or a magic bullet to cure every problem that we have. It is not a guarantee that we will spend our years on this earth in comfort and pleasure. It promises no prosperity other than riches in heaven[4] (which may be very hard to spend here).

Believing in Christ means that you cannot have it both ways. You cannot continually worry about getting your own way, pleasing yourself, and satisfying your appetites, and still have God as Lord and Master. Something has to go. That something is self-rule, and it is a very hard thing to let go of.

The language of Christ and the Bible makes it very clear that a person cannot sit undecided on the fence of salvation. People are clearly on God's side of the fence or they are on the other. For those who refuse to decide, the choice is already made.

Consider the narrowness which Jesus teaches: "You are neither cold nor hot. I wish you were either one or the other! So, because you are lukewarm—neither hot nor cold—I am about to spit you out of my mouth"[5] and "He who is not with me is against me."[6] Obviously Jesus does not accept partial loyalty.

The church building may contain those who are trying to be in the middle. They want to have a bit of God when they need Him, and to have the world the rest of the time. But these people will not be found in the real Church. The real Church is incapable of containing them because they do not really want to follow Christ, they do not really believe.

(Note: There are some Christians who have gone back on their commitment to Christ at some point in their lives. These people are in a completely different situation than those who have never really made a sincere commitment. More about them in chapter 9.)

Because of the commitment He requires, following Christ can be costly and even difficult at times. No one should become a believer without considering the seriousness of that belief and whether they want a relationship with God badly enough to pay the price.

It is a very brave thing to follow the teachings of Christ. Others may ridicule you or gleefully wait for you to stumble and fall. It can be difficult when people who call themselves Christians show up in the spotlight acting like clowns and we are held guilty by association because we also claim the name "Christian."

It is a brave thing to follow Christ because it usually means going against the tide of what everybody else is doing or thinking. A Christian must obey God whether or not His commands are fashionable.

It is a brave thing to be a follower of Christ because a Christian is embarking on a life-long journey. The journey starts with the first step of faith and then must continue sometimes over very difficult terrain. It is a journey to a place where we have never been and cannot really quite imagine. It is a journey made easier by the support of fellow Christians.

Depending upon which local church or denomination you attend and what their particular teachings are, there may be different things expected of you after you put your trust in Jesus Christ. Some Christians will want you to be baptized right away, others will want you to join in Communion, attend a class for new believers, or walk to the front of the church to make your decision a public one. But regardless of what your particular church thinks you should do right after you become a Christian, they all would agree that the most important thing, the vital element, is the choice to make God the boss of your life in the everyday things as well as the big decisions.

Jennifer slid out of the pew that Sunday afternoon and put on her imitation Christian smile. She greeted several people on the way to her car and then slipped behind the wheel. Jennifer muttered a curse under her breath at no one in particular, just to clear the air of the sanctimonious tinge of religion. She started the car and wheeled out of the driveway.

An hour later the police pulled her lifeless body out of the wreckage of her car. No one knew exactly what distraction caused her to plummet off the edge of the road.

They held her funeral at the church on the corner of Main and Ash. It was a cloudless Thursday morning. The pews were filled with mourners. The Pastor gave a message full of soothing reassurance. "Jennifer," he said, "was standing in full joy before the throne of the Lord." The words were nice and well-intended, but they were not true. For as he spoke Jennifer was continuing on the path she had chosen, the broad road away from the face of God, through the grey, the timeless, joyless land where the thirst is never completely quenched.

DISCUSSION QUESTIONS

What makes the difference between a person who is a Christian on the outside only and a person who is a Christian on the inside?

What common beliefs connect all Christians?

What things seem to be the most important to you judging from the time and attention you invest in them? How well does your commitment (or lack of commitment) to God compete with the other priorities in your life?

What are some of the challenges you have faced as you try to follow Christ? What has helped you maintain and grow in your faith in Christ? What influences in the world make being a Christian challenging?

NOTES
1. Leviticus 18:22; also 1 Corinthians 6:9
2. Matthew 6:24
3. Ephesians 2:8,9
4. Matthew 6:19-21
5. Revelation 3:15,16
6. Matthew 12:30

THREE
AVOIDING INFECTIONS

Flee the evil desires of youth, and pursue righteousness, faith, love and peace, along with those who call on the Lord out of a pure heart. 2 Timothy 2:22

For the grace of God . . . . teaches us to say "No" to ungodliness and worldly passions, and to live self-controlled, upright and godly lives. Titus 2:11,12

In four years, from 1347 to 1351, 75 million Europeans died in a plague epidemic from a disease they called the Black Death. Most of those people did not have to die. The Black Death is a disease spread by fleas and rats which flourished in the unsanitary squalor of medieval cities. Trash disposal and cleanliness that is routine in the twentieth century could have saved the lives of millions. But these practices were unknown in fourteenth-century Europe.

In 1915 Mary Mallon was placed in permanent detention until her death in 1938. Mary had been employed as a food handler in New York City. Mary also was a typhoid carrier. (Typhoid is an often fatal disease that causes high fevers and intestinal cramps.)

When it was discovered that Mary was the source of a major outbreak of typhoid, she was dismissed from her job. But rather than stay at home or spend time in recovery, she promptly went out and got another job as a food handler.

By the time health authorities caught up with her again, Mary had been the source of nine separate outbreaks of typhoid fever which killed dozens of people. She had successfully dodged recognition by changing her name. When finally apprehended Mary Mallon was given a new name—Typhoid Mary. This name followed her to her grave.

A little more than 100 years ago it was not uncommon for doctors to go directly from examining a corpse or a highly contagious patient to routine examinations of patients with minor complaints—without washing their hands or sterilizing their instruments. Needless to say, the death rate rocketed through the ceiling with these unsanitary practices.

Eventually, one doctor working in a hospital typical of the era suspected a link between the illnesses of his new patients and the unsanitary practices of the medical profession. This doctor required the other physicians under his authority to wash their hands before moving from one patient to another and to place their tools in boiling water before using them. The death rate in this enlightened doctor's hospital ward dropped sharply.

Unfortunately his colleagues did not believe that there was any connection between illness and cleanliness. The pioneering doctor was forced from his post at the hospital for his seemingly bizarre practices. The rest of the doctors at the hospital could then comfortably go on contaminating their trusting patients without interference.

We live in a world ripe with infections. While a few can be good, such as infectious laughter, the vast majority of infections are bad.

In addition to physical or behavioral areas, Christians must be aware that infections may attack in the spiritual realm. Spiritual infections can cripple or destroy our viability as children of God. They can tear down the good things that God is building up in us.

Have you ever noticed how a cold or the flu gets passed from family member to family member? When this occurs the house echoes with coughs and hacks, trash cans fill up with spent tissue, everybody mopes around, and chicken soup seems to be the favorite food. It is especially annoying when family flu epidemics coincide with family celebrations such as birthdays or Christmas. When a bug is making the rounds, people just don't work, play, or act like they are supposed to.

It is similar in the church family. The spiritual illness of one person causes all to be concerned. The spiritual illness of a great many people causes the church to loose its vibrancy and effectiveness. This is particularly true if the spiritual illness is something as contagious as bitterness, gossip, immorality, or backbiting.

Most of the troubles that beset a church (or the individuals in it) are not just carried in on the wind; they have been invited. They are encouraged by people who put themselves in positions of great risk—people who are spiritually ill, who have been infected by impurity in their attitudes or actions.

If trying to stay effective for God is our goal, then we must learn not to allow impurities to enter and breed in our souls. We must, as the Bible says, become pure.[1]

When trying to get this idea across to my youth group I often do a little stunt. Using a can of soda, a glass, and a partially filled trash can as props, I begin by asking if any of the kids would like a soda. Most of them say yes. One person is invited to step up to the front of the room. Before giving him the soda I dump the contents of the trash can onto the floor, pour the drink into the trash can, swish it around, then pour the liquid into the clean glass. Then I offer the bubbly concoction to the volunteer. I have not had one person accept the soda after it has been dirtied in the trash can.

The point is this: most people have no desire to pollute their bodies with filthy substances. In fact, the demonstration I've described often gets a unanimous response, "Yuck!" Yet often we do not have the same reluctance about polluting our minds and hearts.

Most of us realize that certain things do not help us to live as Christians should. We know that it is difficult to keep our sexual impulses under control if we busily ignite them with pictures from *Playboy* magazine or steamy movies. Such preoccupation with cheap sex also makes it difficult for men to view women as anything more than objects to fulfill their desires. Similarly, although romance novels may seem to make men appear heroic, they may cause some women to devalue men, to view men as rescuers who only have value as long as they fulfill their needs.

Usually we do not need anyone to point out the things that disease our souls. But sometimes Christians underestimate the danger and end up in moral peril. Perhaps the following illustration will make this clearer.

I live in Hawaii on the island of Kauai. Each year a half dozen or so people drown in the waters off Kauai. Most of these people are visitors from places that do not have oceans and they get caught in the big winter surf.

During the winter months storms deep in the northern Pacific throw huge walls of water south. Increasing in size as successive storm waves catch up with each other, these walls of water travel until they reach landfall. When they reach the west coast of North America, the long gradually building continental shelf tends to diminish the size and power of the waves. In Hawaii, the swells come out of deep water to smack directly into the islands. The power and force behind these racing mountains of water is staggering.

Unpracticed swimmers die in these seas because they underestimate the power of the pretty blue wave rolling towards them and because they are overly confident of their own skill and ability. (Just because a person swims a mile each day in a pool back home, doesn't mean that he or she is in the kind of shape necessary to tackle big winter surf.)

But undaunted by warnings, dozens of inexperienced people march out to get the drubbing of their lives. Most of them make it back to shore, although some have to be dragged in by rescuers. But a few unfortunates get the final lesson in avoiding dangerous situations.

Life is full of potentially dangerous situations. Some do not threaten us physically, but are deadly threats to our spiritual survival.

For example, to invite your boyfriend over to spend the evening with you while you baby-sit can be a way to get to know each other, a chance to spend time together away from parents or siblings. But it can also be very dangerous to your virtue, especially if one or both of you struggle with sexual temptation.

Some Christians purposefully put themselves in situations that threaten their morals. They get a thrill from coming as close to sin as possible. They ignore the Bible teaching to flee temptation[2] and hang out with a bunch of sleazy toads who have reputations for trouble. They try to bail out just before getting involved in something that is clearly immoral. These Christians put themselves in tempting situations over and over again in a game of spiritual Russian roulette. Sooner or later—BOOM—the players will find themselves with a spiritual life that is shot to pieces.

To remain free from spiritual disease it is important to be as serious about taking precautions around those who are infected with sin as you would around someone carrying typhoid or plague.

The recent AIDS epidemic has led people who give first aid to be extra cautious about contagion. Many police officers and medics are given rubber gloves and special mouthpieces to wear when administering first aid to automobile accident victims. The scenes of accidents are often bloody and there is no way of telling which victims may carry the AIDS virus. The precautions of using rubber gloves and mouth pieces are an attempt to protect rescue workers while they perform their duty for those suffering. The idea is to put a layer of insulation between the care givers and the potentially infected victim. This same kind of strategy can protect Christians from deadly spiritual infections.

The Bible gives Christians guidelines to help act as insulation between their spiritual purity and the sin that is so widespread in the secular world. One such guideline advises "Do not be yoked together with unbelievers."[3] A yoke is a collar that is used to hold together a team of oxen or horses as they work pulling wagons or ploughs. Christians are not to be bound together in this way with non-Christians. This Bible passage is most often applied to marriage. But it could also be applied to business dealings, going steady, or to cooperating with false teachers. Christians are not supposed to enter into important partnerships with non-Christians. Christians' deep relationships should be with other Christians. This insulates them from being overly influenced by philosophies or values that are against the teachings of the Bible.

Another guideline is to "set you minds on things above."[4] In other words make sure that we are in a solid, growing relationship with God. Augustine, a great bishop of the early church said, "Love God with all your heart, soul, and mind. Then do whatever you want." Augustine meant that when our hearts and minds are clearly focused on God, our choices and decisions will not be against His perfect will.

Of course to keep our hearts centered on God is a tough thing to do. We mess things up a lot. But all we need to do is to tell God that we have messed up and He will get us "scrubbed up" again.[5]

A third thing that Christians can do to help prevent spiritual infection is to build up our spiritual immune systems. In our physical bodies there are guardians in our blood streams. These guardians are called T-cells, white blood corpuscles, and antibodies. They go on alert if any strange invaders go floating by. The guardians attack in force any microbes that might endanger the well-being of our bodies. Most of the time the guardian forces win. When they are in the midst of a battle we know it because we feel sick. Most of the symptoms of illness come from the battle being raged. We feel so crummy because our bodies are being used as a battlefield. When the guardians lose, the body dies.

Fortunately modern science has developed some powerful weapons to give the guardians a big advantage. Antibiotics such as penicillin have saved countless lives by throwing extra weapons into the battle.

Building up our spiritual immune systems can be done by keeping our prayer lives in good condition, by reading God's Word, the Bible, and by stretching our minds with Christian reading materials. To be strong Christians we need to know what we believe and why we believe it. We need to have fellow Christians we can go to for encouragement, wisdom, and insight.

Christians need to take precautions around those involved in sin. We need to know our limits and weaknesses and we need to build up our spiritual weapons. But this does not mean that we are to retreat from the wreckage of the world. We are to dig through the rubble for survivors.

Jesus did not separate Himself from the world. He dined with the most vilely infected sinners in town. He touched the unclean. He was not aloof like the other religious leaders of His day. He did have a circle of close friends, the Twelve, who were righteous men. But Jesus was in touch with those who needed desperately to hear the good news He had come to preach.

It would be a mistake to suggest (as some Christians have) that we should have nothing to do with those who are not believers. On the contrary, we should get to know non-Christians and hope to win their respect. Through us they may get the desire to know our Master.

The late Joseph Bayly wrote a hilarious satire called

The Gospel Blimp. The story is about a Christian couple's concern for a neighbor couple who are unsaved. The Christians share their concern with their local church. The congregation decides to do something about it.

The tale goes on to show how the church members, trying to evangelize without touching the sinner, finally buy a large blimp complete with blinking light messages of salvation and loudspeakers to blare gospel meditations. Members of the Church Blimp Committee make aerial passes over the home of the non-Christians interrupting their television programs with noise and static. They bomb the backyard of the unsaved couple with bundles of tracts as the husband tries to mow his lawn. (The tracts clog the lawn mower.) These well-meaning but ineffective Christians make a general nuisance of themselves. Of course the members of the Blimp Committee feel that they are doing the job of evangelism.

As the story draws to a close, the Christian couple whose concern started the whole blimp affair decide to make friends with the neighbors. The men play golf together. The women share friendship.

By the end of the book the neighbors have been converted to Christianity not by the wild escapades of the Gospel Blimp but by the simple friendship and caring of a Christian couple.

Bayly's message is clear. It is wrong to separate ourselves from those who are not Christians. It is our duty to administer Christ's love to them.

But we must be balanced in the time we spend with non-Christians and with brothers and sisters in the Lord. Spending too much time with non-Christians can cause us to accept standards that fall short of Christ's teaching. But if we have no contact with non-Christians we can become out of touch with their needs and with what is going on in our culture.

There may be times when it is important for a person to break all of his or her ties with things that confuse or disrupt their spiritual health. This can mean that there will be times that Christians need to reduce their contact with non-Christians. For instance, believers going through periods of doubt would do well to hang out with fellow believers who can encourage them. If a Christian has a problem with alcohol abuse he or she would be better avoiding places where alcohol is served. God may want to take some people out of circulation in worldly circles for a time to give them a chance to grow and mature as believers.

But whether we move in largely Christian circles or most of our contacts are with non-Christians, as believers we are all members of the Body of Christ—the Church. And, ultimately, it is the personal uprightness of each member of the Church that gives the Church credibility. If many of the church members are living a dynamic Christian life, that will bring strength and vitality into the Body. If a local church is full of spiritual weaklings, it will probably be characterized by pettiness, anger, and distrust.

An army that is sick cannot be expected to do much good in battle. A church whose members are spiritually unhealthy will have a hard time "fighting the good fight."[6] It all starts with individual Christians and their efforts to avoid spiritual infections.

DISCUSSION QUESTIONS

What are some subtle ways impurity can creep into the heart of a Christian?

44 THE CHURCH

Describe a situation where you resisted the temptation to do something wrong. How could yielding to that temptation have been harmful to your spiritual health?

Think of another situation that you feel would be threatening to your spiritual health. Why would that situation be dangerous?

What steps can you take to protect yourself from influences that may come between you and your relationship to Jesus Christ?

Why is it important that a Christian protect himself or herself from impurity?

NOTES
1. 1 John 3:3
2. 2 Timothy 2:22
3. 2 Corinthians 6:14
4. Colossians 3:2
5. 1 John 1:9
6. 1 Timothy 1:18

FOUR
THE GILDED TRAP

For the love of money is a root of all kinds of evil. Some people, eager for money, have wandered from the faith and pierced themselves with many griefs. 1 Timothy 6:10

Gene proudly guided his shining new Mercedes into the church parking lot. A small rusting wreck pulled into the space next to him. He winced as he saw the dented door of the compact car swung out by the chubby arms of a tousle-haired kid. The old door came dangerously close to the perfect paint job of the luxury sedan.

Gene waited in his car as kids piled out of the rust bucket next to him. He tapped his fingers impatiently on his exotic steering wheel as the urchins outside discovered the joy of viewing their distorted images in the brilliantly reflective polish of his car. He muttered "brats" under his breath when he sensed several of them had left their greasy handprints on his fender.

The driver of the small car, a weary-looking woman with well-worn shoes and clothing, finally rounded up the last of her brood and shuffled them along the sidewalk to Sunday School.

Gene inhaled a final whiff of leather trimmed interior as he slid out of his car. He walked to the opposite side of the magnificent vehicle and with his linen handkerchief carefully wiped off the smudges he found there.

Gene put his Bible under his arm and marched into

morning worship. He was a man who was proud that he had been able to provide the "good life" for his family, a man whose responsibility and industry had paid off, a man who thought that his responsibilities to his family ended at his front door. Gene could not see that the poor single mother who pulled up next to him in the church parking lot and her scruffy brood were part of the family too—the family of God.

What is the gravest danger to the Church in the Western world today? Drugs and alcohol abuse? The threat of communism? The apalling lack of morality in our society? Probably not. It is very likely that our affluence is the greatest danger. Wealth is a gilded trap. It is, like most traps, very subtle. But it's punch is powerful and deadly.

It may be helpful to consider for a moment the anatomy of a trap. Most traps do not advertise their purpose. A snare is placed among the bushes along with vines and shrubbery. A mousetrap looks similar to other bits of wood and metal that a mouse might encounter in a garage or workshop. A bear trap is always covered with leaves to camouflage its deadly teeth. So, if affluence is like a trap, we should expect to have to search for its dangerous characteristics. How the love of money corrupts a person's soul, how it makes them care little for other human beings may be hidden. We should not expect to witness the quiet workings of greed on the character of a person. We probably will not see broadcast the story of those whose lives and families have been destroyed while they reached for the golden ring. These sights may be concealed by a polished exterior, but they are there.

The thing that might catch our eye is the bait. Traps

generally contain bait that is good in itself, but which is in the midst of something harmful. The cheese in the mousetrap is food. The meat in a spring trap is what most fur animals are hungry for and need. The bait is rarely the problem.

Likewise, money by itself is not a problem. Jesus said, "The worker deserves his wages."[1] But money, like bait, can often be found in the midst of situations that are deadly spiritually. It is not money but the *love of money* that is "a root of all kinds of evil."[2] For the love of money people may sacrifice everything: friends, family, honor, morals, and their relationship with God. They may find themselves alone in the gilded trap.

Traps vary. Some traps snap suddenly, some slowly squeeze their victims. Almost all traps give their victims what they came to get—as well as something they did not expect to receive. Some traps give a bit of freedom, usually the length of chain that connects the trap to its anchor. But in the end, the sense of freedom is just an illusion.

The love of money works differently on each person. Some get their first taste of materialism and are hopelessly hooked. Their wills are broken with a snap and they become the willing slaves of money and the things it can buy. Others find themselves getting further and further into a situation where there seems to be no way out. The debts mount up and chasing money seems to be the only recourse.

Most traps leave their victims as prey to other predators. Obviously if an animal is trapped, and the trapper does not return to claim his victim, other hungry animals will find an easy meal.

The love of money can leave us defenseless against other hungry carnivores of the soul. It can leave us exhausted from trying to free ourselves from our payments or from our efforts to make enough to buy a BMW or jet skis. The struggle to make money may take every minute of the day. We may no longer have time to fellowship with other Christians or spend time getting to know God. This spiritual starvation can cause us to make wrong choices in other situations and complicate our lives even more.

The use of money is often misguided because it is almost entirely self-directed. Most people rarely use it to do good outside their small circle of family or friends.

While it is natural and good to use money to take care of our human needs of hunger and comfort, the average Christian in industrialized societies usually goes beyond needs deep into the area of luxury.

Another problem with money is that it is often equated with power. The desire for it motivates people to do detestable things. This power money wields in each of us is probably much stronger than we like to admit. For example, how much money would it take to get you to take a big drink of sour milk? Not for ten dollars? How about $100? Is there a price that would lure you to change your mind and act against your normal reactions? If so, then you, like the majority of people who answer this question honestly, are far more attracted to money than you might like to believe.

In Western society money is seen as an indicator of success. It is viewed by many guys as the ticket needed to get the gorgeous girl of their dreams and by many women as the pathway to beauty and security. People are judged successes not on the basis of their characters, but on the basis of their bank accounts.

Money confuses judgment. It is difficult to remain

impartial if you find out that one of your friends is a multimillionaire. Most of us favor those whose "magic" might rub off on us or who are in a position to reward our friendship.

To favor a person because he or she is wealthy (or famous, or attractive) goes against Bible teaching.[3] It is shameful that many church leaders have courted the wealthy in their congregation because they know the special attention will be rewarded in the offering plate. Yet, we all struggle with the tendency to favor the rich.

Money doesn't last. The things it can buy are temporary. They rust and break down; they go out of style or become obsolete. Money can be stolen or lost on the stock market. It can lose its value or be declared worthless. If it is hoarded and never used, it is simply paper or metal with potential.

Money can even have a nasty way of disappearing. Recently an acquaintance of mine, who had fallen on particularly hard times, sold a piece of property and managed to end up with $7 thousand profit on the deal. He was paid in cash. The money was placed in an envelope. This gentleman stopped at a pay phone outside the local market. He took his envelope of cash with him rather than leave it unguarded in the car. For whatever reason, because the phone call upset him or because of the stress he was under, when he walked away from the phone booth he left the envelope sitting on the ledge inside. A few miles down the road the man realized his mistake and raced back to the phone booth. The envelope was gone. His forgetfulness had made someone's day—but thoroughly ruined his own.

An abundance of money can desensitize our reliance on God. People may feel that there is no need to trust God when the cupboards are filled with food and the safe is awash in jewels.

A life filled with the pursuit of money or the safeguarding of it can cause personal values to become twisted as the following true story illustrates.

Henrietta "Hettie" Green sat down to her daily meal of cold oatmeal. In a neighboring clinic her son lay in bed twisting in agony from a recently performed amputation of his leg. His unfortunate condition was the result of too much time being wasted searching for a free clinic in which to treat his injury. Before his mother could secure the clinic, the boy's leg was beyond saving. A tragedy of poverty? Hardly, Hettie Green had $11 million in the bank. Her estate was valued at $95 million. She was simply a miserly, twisted old woman who cared more about money than she did about people—including her own son.

It is interesting to note that Jesus often dealt with the topic of money. He realized its magnetism and pull. He saw its ability to corrupt. One of the marks of a mature Christian is freedom from the love of money.

Several years ago a young couple from the United States tried to adopt two young girls from an orphanage south of the border. The couple thought that the director of the orphanage would be thrilled to see the children placed in a loving and affluent home, miles away from the dust, sweat, and filth of the border town of the little orphanage.

When approached about the opportunity and desire of this couple, the director of the orphanage, a Mexican woman with a robust faith in Christ, buried her chin in her hand. A thoughtful but distressed look crossed her face. The couple, sensing something was wrong asked in stumbling Spanish if the idea was not a good one.

The director slowly explained that she thought the affluence of the United States would be bad for the spiritual development of the children. She said, "Look in your country. You have everything. You have so many distractions to draw you away from putting your trust in the Lord. Here, we have nothing. We must depend on Christ just for the food to eat and the clothes to wear on our backs. It is easier to trust in Christ when you have nothing than when you are surrounded by so much."

The couple understood her point of view. They could see that from her vantage point an abundance of things was not a blessing, but a curse. The couple still thought that the children would have a better standard of living being raised in the United States, but they could see the threat to spiritual growth that affluence can bring.

One of the reasons that affluence is so dangerous is that we do not sense its grip on us. We have come to see our luxuries as necessities. Still worse, we have deluded ourselves into thinking that our material abundance is a sign of God's blessing, that He must approve our luxurious spending. If abundance is an indication of God's blessing and approval, then He certainly blessed a number of questionable persons and governments throughout history, including some who did everything in their power to stomp out His name.

If the love of money is a trap, what can Christians do to make sure they are not snared? They can do a great many things, but many of them will be painful.

One thing Christians can do is to settle for second best. With few exceptions, there is little reason to own an expensive sports car or a fabulous stereo system. In many areas we can settle for things that cost far less than the newest model. Naturally there are exceptions. For instance, when buying glasses you may wish to get the finest lenses you can buy in order to protect your sight. But the desire to get diamond trimmed frames reflects a totally different motivation.

We can use the money we save through wise or moderate spending to do good for others. An economy car for a struggling family can be bought with the difference in price of a cheaper model sports car and the top-of-the-line model. Glasses for a poor child can be bought with the money saved on the purchase of plain instead of jeweled frames. If all the Church began to spend this way it would shake the earth for the gospel.

Imagine a church where businessmen loaned struggling young families the down payment for their own homes, without interest, for a few years until they were able to afford to pay them back. Imagine a church where cars, refrigerators, sofas, and other household goods suddenly appeared on the doorsteps or in the driveways of needy church or community members.

A dream? Perhaps. But is it no less of a dream than many of the other ideals of Christianity? In reality it is in our power to be that kind of Church, if we are not too trapped by our own self-indulgent affluence.

In the beginning of this chapter we spoke of Gene and his Mercedes Benz. If Gene really cared about others in his Christian family how might his life be different for him and those around him? Perhaps Gene would have purchased a less expensive car. Perhaps he would have purchased two of them and donated one to the struggling single mother driving the smoking rust bucket. Perhaps he would have cared less for his shiny car and more for the condition of the people who worshiped with him. Perhaps he would have seen that his responsibility to his family includes not just those at home but those in the family of Christ.

Perhaps, but Gene had his hand deep in the gilded trap. His property was his badge. But it was also his curse. His "treasure" would someday lie upon the junk heap, but the little treasures piling out of the old car next to him would live on and on for eternity. Now, there is an investment.

DISCUSSION QUESTIONS

At what point does wealth become a problem for the Church? What are the symptoms of this problem?

How does the love of money affect your life right now?

What kinds of bait seem most appealing to you?

As a Christian, what can reduce the power of the love of money in your life?

How will control over the power of the love of money in your life affect the way you relate to people in your church and community?

NOTES
1. Luke 10:7
2. 1 Timothy 6:10
3. James 2:1

FIVE
THE SHEPHERD

Those who have served well gain an excellent standing and great assurance in their faith in Christ Jesus. 1 Timothy 3:13

As cute as they may look in storybooks and on Christmas cards, sheep are among the dumbest animals that exist. They seldom know what is best for themselves and seem concerned only with eating on the hillside all day. Jesus may not have meant the comparison of His followers to sheep as a compliment. But whether or not it is a complimentary comparison, it is accurate.

In many ways we humans are not all that smart. Like sheep, we often do not know what is best for us. Or if we do know, we may not act on the knowledge. Like sheep, we are followers. But we often follow for the wrong reasons. We may follow a person who satisfies our desire for praise, acceptance, or fun. Or we may follow our sexual urges or appetite for food. Some people are led by a lust for money or power. But we all follow someone or something. It is no wonder we need a Wise Shepherd to lead us. That Shepherd is Jesus.[1]

Interestingly, God has seen fit to assign the job of "under shepherd" or "assistant shepherd" to some of His sheep. We call these people "pastors," which in the original language means "shepherd." Pastors are not the Great Shepherd.[2] That title is reserved for Christ alone. But pastors are supposed to be like sheep who have heard and understood the instructions of the Great Shepherd and are trying to get the other sheep to pay attention to those instructions.

When the flock is united in following God's instructions the results are dramatic. The earth-shaking power of the Church comes from God working through the lives of the individual believers who together make up the Church. This power has been the force behind history-changing events such as the abolition of slavery in the United States and the children's rights movement in England. Christians fleeing persecution founded the United States. Christian thought has influenced the art, literature, and culture of a great portion of the world. While the strength of an individual Christian may be substantial, the collective strength of the Body of Christ is unbreakable, very much like the difference in strength between a rope and its individual fibers.

The Church would not have so much strength and influence were it not organized and guided by God. God has given the Church guidelines for organization. Groups of believers, while led by the Holy Spirit, are also under the guidance of at least one overseer/elder.

There are many words used to describe the person who leads a church. Reverend, pastor, priest, minister, elder, clergyman, brother, preacher, and chaplain are just some of them. In most churches the leaders are on a paid staff. Their job is to work with the people of the church to run the church programs and to be spiritual advisers.

Of course a person does not have to be paid to be the overseer of a church. Almost all of the leaders of the early church were people from within the Body of Believers who were recognized for their spiritual example and wisdom. Most of these people were employed outside the church.

Some churches today, usually in rural locations, are

still led by pastors who are employed outside the church and who are not paid a salary for preaching. Often these leaders are local church people who have had no special schooling but who are dedicated and have been recognized for their Bible understanding.

It is a mistake to think that a person must go to Bible school or seminary in order to shepherd a group of people; the Scripture indicates no such requirement. But many churches insist that their leaders have a seminary education as protection against being led by someone who is unprepared, who believes unbiblical doctrines, or who is a big flake. Some groups of Christians protest that formal training is not as important as having the heart of a pastor—a spiritual gift.[3]

Many groups of Christians have ceremonies called "ordinations" to recognize God's call on a person to the role of shepherd. Many Bible scholars believe that it was Timothy's ordination Paul referred to when he said, "The body of elders laid their hands on you."[4] Laying on of hands (placing hands on the head, shoulders, or back of a person while praying for him) is a common element of ordination ceremonies. But the ceremony is not so important as making certain that God has chosen the person being ordained.

The Bible lays down some very strict qualifications for overseers. The guidelines apply whether leaders are paid workers or volunteers. The qualifications cover not only how shepherds lead but also how they conduct their personal lives.[5] This makes sense. The goal is to have leaders who can show us by their actions that living the Christian life is possible, practical, beneficial, and even enjoyable.

Because of their position of responsibility and example, many pastors are seen as holy men who are

THE SHEPHERD 59

untouched by the hurts, cares, and temptations of the world. Probably nothing is further from the truth. If anything, temptations are even greater for some people in leadership. There is a saying that helps to explain one reason why this is true: "The bigger the targets the bigger guns Satan uses to hit them."

One pastor shared with me a situation that is common: he has to be extremely cautious with his counseling appointments with women. He keeps the door of his office open and makes sure his secretary is in her place just outside his door. Why? Because over the last few years he has had at least a dozen women, hurting for one reason or another, try to initiate an affair with him. The open door and the church secretary are both preventive measures to discourage women from suggesting improper conduct. The presence of the secretary also protects against any false stories that might be spread about the pastor if no one knew what was going on in his office.

This situation is not a problem that confronts only men. A married women who is also a children's minister told me about an ugly rumor that was circulating about her at church. It seems that she got a phone call at the church office from a despondent man. He asked her to see him during his lunch hour. The man was suicidal and desperately needed to talk to someone. Wanting to help, the minister met him for lunch. Tears rolled down the man's cheeks as he poured out his problems. The minister gently held his hand, comforting him, as she explained the love and hope of Jesus. Just then three members of the parish walked into the restaurant and right by the table where the children's minister and the man sat. They didn't stop to say hello. The minister thought the parishioners were being courteous by not interrupting what obviously was an emotional counseling session. She was stunned several days later when confronted by a church member who demanded an explanation of her behavior. After all, three people had seen her breaking up with her lover!

It may seem odd that people try to tempt or spread rumors about their ministers. But some people feel so guilty and rotten about themselves that they want to bring others down to their level. This reassures them that they are not really so different or so bad. Other people see the pastor of a church, particularly a large church, as a great target or even a "turn on."

There is plenty of sickness in the world and ministers see more of it than do most other people. This is why being a minister can be a very difficult and tiring job.

Shepherds serve in the world, in society, not just behind church walls. But people often act funny if they find out that one of the people in the crowd or at the party is a minister.

Pastor Tom was relaxing at the beach with several high school kids from his church. Tom was a youthful minister who enjoyed water sports with the same relish as did the kids in his youth group.

Other students from the high school joined Tom and his group on the sand. Most of them knew each other from school. A young man began talking about his latest adventure using a volley of four-letter words and highly descriptive references to the human anatomy. After a few minutes one of the students bumped the young man and whispered to him that the tanned fellow sitting close by was a pastor.

The young man's face turned ashen. Feeling like a fool, he mumbled an apology and quickly excused himself from the group. Obviously, he knew that his speech was wrong.

The presence of Pastor Tom served as a splash of cold water on a fiery tongue, a reminder to a straying sheep that God is looking for him.

One of the reasons the young man was so embarrassed was that like many people, he felt that ministers have very high standards and he did not want to offend Pastor Tom. Most ministers do have high standards—the biblical qualifications for their position in the church.

In Paul's letter to Timothy he said that one of the qualifications for overseers was that they must be "the husband of but one wife." Through the years there have been different interpretations of this passage. Some feel that it means that a person must have only one spouse in his or her lifetime. This excludes anyone who has ever been divorced for any reason from serving as a pastor. Others feel that it has more to do with a historical setting in which some who became Christians were polygamous (had several wives). The people who hold this view see the Bible passage as a rule against polygamy. Another common interpretation is that Paul was saying that it means that pastors should be men (husband) and not women and that these men should have only one wife. Still others believe that the passage is a general affirmation of the importance of faithfulness in marriage, whether the overseer is a man or a woman.

The other qualifications for an overseer (pastor) give us a picture of a person who is sensible and sensitive: above reproach, temperate, self-controlled, respectable, hospitable, able to teach, not given to drunkenness, not violent but gentle, not quarrelsome, not a lover of money. He must manage his family well, must not be a recent convert, and should have a good reputation with outsiders.[6] The church leader must really have his life under control.

We all want our leaders to make sound decisions and to keep their promises. We want our pastors to have the kind of self-control that will make them examples of godliness, not models for the cover of the *National Enquirer*. If our pastors have the biblical qualifications of being above reproach, temperate, and self-controlled we will probably not have to worry about being embarrassed by their behavior.

A pastor is supposed to like people. He must be hospitable. He must be a true friend to believers. He should go out of his way to reach out to new people, people who may not quite fit in with the rest of the flock, foreigners, or visitors. A pastor must be an example of warmth and friendship to all people if they expect the rest of the people who make up the church to do the same.

Most of us are used to seeing the pastor of a church up in a pulpit delivering a sermon. Did you know that one of the qualifications for being an overseer is that he should not bore you to tears? You bet! A pastor is supposed to be a capable and qualified teacher. And a teacher hasn't taught until someone has learned. Of course some lessons or sermons are not directed at young people but at adults. But a good teacher will try to communicate the important ideas they have discovered to his students in the most effective way possible. This is a tough assignment for preachers!

The qualification that an overseer must be temperate means that he must not be chemically dependent. This means that he cannot be addicted to alcohol or drugs. The reasons for this qualification are pretty obvious. Use of substances interferes with the maturing process and with the ability to reason, listen, learn, concentrate, focus, judge, and feel sympathy. Substance abuse interferes with every aspect of pastoring.

A pastor is not supposed to be the kind of person who is violent. He should not pick fights (verbal or physical) or have a "chip on his shoulder." Instead of quarreling he should be the kind of person who tries to bring harmony into relationships.

The Bible says that an overseer should not be addicted to money. (Many congregations help their pastors avoid this addiction by giving him a very small salary.) Most of us don't want to donate money to the church to enrich individuals. We want our funds to go to help run church programs and to make life a little easier for those who are truly needy. If a money-hungry person was pastoring our church, we would probably distrust him. We might even quit giving or we might funnel our contributions into another ministry.

The qualification that a pastor must manage his family well has some interesting applications. One is the one given in the Bible: "If anyone does not know how to manage his own family, how can he take care of God's church?"[7] In other words, a shepherd who cannot effectively discipline his own kids will probably have a problem with church discipline. A person who cannot lead his family probably will not be able to lead others. A person who cannot manage the business of running a family will probably not be able to manage the much more complicated business of running a church.

The leader of a church is not to be a new convert to the faith. While a new believer often has vitality, fresh ideas, and lots of contagious excitement, they do not have the depth of experience that comes with having walked with Jesus for many years. They do not have the background of Bible knowledge nor have they had to wrestle with many tough issues the way an experienced believer has. The new convert has not had time to show that he will be faithful even when it hurts. And faithfulness is essential in Christian leaders. The Bible also says that new converts may become conceited. They may be overly impressed with their own role in becoming a member of God's family and not understand that God alone deserves the praise. A new believer may have a whole lot of his old nature still alive and well. A place of authority in the Body is just what that old sinful nature might be looking for, not so much to serve Jesus as to serve his own pride.

Another interesting qualification for overseers is that they should have a good reputation with those outside the church. This means that the example of Christ in their lives must be so genuine and transparent that even those who do not believe in Jesus will think of pastors as decent chaps. People who have demonstrated to the world that they are bozos or bimbos need not apply to lead God's sheep.

As you can see, it is tough to be in the role of a pastor or overseer. It is very demanding and the only people available to fill the job are human just like you and me. As you watch your pastor on Sunday morning try to remember that he has a temper, desires, and bad traits. He struggles with a sinful nature like any other person. He sometimes may not feel appreciated. He may sometimes wait until the last minute to work on his message (and it shows). He may have times when he seems to be blind to the things that need to get done around the church or to attitudes that need to be changed. In the end he is accountable to God for a great deal. For in becoming your shepherd he has become responsible for guiding the flock. He must listen carefully to the Great Shepherd or he will be on dangerous ground.

You can do things to make your pastor's job easier. You can look for things to do to help. You can tell him when you like the service. Tell him what you like about what he does. You can call him up and invite him to lunch to get to know him. Most shepherds will try to turn the conversation around to talk about you; that is their nature. But don't let him do it. For a change talk about him. You might be surprised to find out that the shepherd is also a really neat guy!

DISCUSSION QUESTIONS

In what ways do Christians act like sheep?

Why do you think God uses people to guide His sheep? Write a description of the kind of person you think God might choose to help His flock?

What pressures or influences in modern society might make it difficult for an overseer to live up to the standards God has given for this position?

How can we support and encourage those who shepherd us?

NOTES
1. John 10:14
2. Hebrews 13:20
3. Ephesians 4:11
4. 1 Timothy 4:14
5. 1 Timothy 3:2-13; Titus 1:6-9
6. 1 Timothy 3:2-7
7. 1 Timothy 3:5

SIX
WOMEN IN THE CHURCH

I do not permit a woman to teach or to have authority over a man. 1 Timothy 2:12

There is neither Jew nor Greek, slave nor free, male nor female, for you are all one in Christ Jesus. Galatians 3:28

Eileen wanted to start a church. This had been her unswerving desire for many years as she trained in Bible college and seminary. Now that she was through with her education, Eileen was anxious to put roots down in the little bedroom community where she moved following graduation. She wanted to get to work.

Eileen decided to start holding church services in the living room of her apartment. For a week she stomped through her neighborhood. Going door-to-door she introduced herself and invited all those she met to stop by if they did not have a church home. Eileen made certain her listeners understood that the first service of the new church would be held on the following Sunday.

That Sunday Eileen made a pot of coffee, spread out a plate of homemade cookies and waited anxiously for the congregation to arrive. No one came.

Discouraged but not about to quit, Eileen placed ads in all of the local papers and tramped through the neighborhood again. Again there was no turnout on Sunday morning.

As Eileen shared her frustrations over the phone with

a woman friend she was surprised to hear this remark: "Eileen, has the thought ever occurred to you that maybe your neighborhood isn't ready for a woman pastor?"

"But how do they know what I'm like unless they try me?" protested Eileen.

"That's beside the point," her friend replied. "They don't sound like they want a woman pastor—even if she is good!"

More than half of the readers of this chapter are women. If you are one of them you may disagree with some of the things that you are going to read. Some of you may completely and wholeheartedly agree. Some of you may get angry about situations that were and still are commonly found in churches. Even as the words are being written for this chapter the expectations and opportunities for women's involvement in the Church are thawing in some locations and freezing in others. Christians as individuals and as church bodies do not agree on what women's roles should be. Many see this as a reflection of modern society.

Our society sends confusing messages about many things, particularly roles for women in the work place, church, and home. This confusion may have spilled over into the Church. As in the case with other questions on how we should live, Christians search the Bible for answers about women's roles. But even though there are some solid concepts presented in the Bible about this subject, there is very much that is not said. And Christians do not always agree on how to interpret what is said. For instance one Bible passage discussed in the previous chapter says that overseers (pastors) are to be the husbands of one wife.[1] To some Christians this clearly says that church leaders are to be male since only men are husbands. Other

Christians believe that this passage stresses marital fidelity, not the sex of the leader.

When unsure about an issue, Christians often take cues for the appropriateness of things from the culture in which they live. So, for example, if most women in society wear hats and white gloves to important occasions, it follows that the church will think that it is good taste and appropriate dignity for women to wear hats and white gloves in church gatherings. When hats and gloves go out of fashion, which is what happens of course, then it is appropriate to go to church gatherings without them.

There is nothing in Scripture about hats and gloves being the correct thing to wear when worshipping (veils maybe, but not pillbox hats). But when they were in style, many people would have been offended and considered a woman inappropriately dressed if she appeared for church services without them.

This is kind of the long way around to explain that there are many ideas that we may feel very strongly about but which have little biblical support. Many of these ideas are strongly tied to our culture. Some of these ideas have to do with women. As Christians we must try to see through the cultural smog to find God's truth. This can be especially difficult after a long history of influence.

Sadly, throughout history many societies have treated women very shabbily. Sometimes women were seen as property rather than people (in a few places in the world women are still seen in this light). Naturally the treatment of women often depended on the particular culture or tribe, but it is safe to say that women have often been powerless. Because men were the warriors, providers, and guardians, women often had no choice but to give them the leadership.

Often people with power treat those they control badly. Men with power have not only treated women badly but have also treated poorly any men they didn't like. Interestingly, on the occasions when women did gain power they did not treat people any better than their male counterparts. Nor did these powerful women do anything significant to bring change to their sisters.

Women have suffered oppression from the hands of both men and women. People who feel they have been oppressed often get angry. This is exactly what some women feel today—angry.

What all of this has to do with the Church is simple. The Church is being asked to decide what roles and duties a woman should be able to assume within the Body of Believers. The problem is, many in the Church are not quite sure. But in spite of the confusion and sometimes even bitter arguments over women's roles, there are a few things that we can all agree on. These things can be viewed as gifts.

One very great gift that God through His Word gives to women is a clear sense of equal value. For although there is not agreement on the jobs or positions women may hold, all Christians agree that women have equal value in Christ. The narratives of Christ's ministry are full of His dealings with women. In contrast with the other religious groups of the period, Jesus was unique in His involvement with women such as Mary and Martha, Mary Magdalene, Joanna, and Susanna who were among His followers and close friends.

The Bible points out with brilliant clarity that in Christ, that is in God's eyes and in the eyes of the Church, there is to be no favoritism based on race, economic status, or sex.[2] This instruction marks a landmark in human rights.

72 THE CHURCH

The Church was not to segregate people by caste systems or by gender. This new attitude of equality raised the position of many women who had been isolated and discriminated against routinely.

The Jews had even marked off sections of the Temple that were off limits to women and to converts from non-Jewish backgrounds. These forbidden sections were closer to the holy of holies and women and Gentiles were not considered worthy of entering them. Christianity swept away these divisions and allowed all people equality and worth before God and each other. Whatever women were considered in the society in which they lived, property or princesses, they became absolutely equal to every other member of the Church. In fact the idea of calling each other "brother" and "sister" was part of the smashing down of class barriers. Now the nobleman was a brother to the slave and the maid a sister to the landowner.

But equality before God is not the only gift He gives to women. Through the Church He gives them something else—something that some of them feel is demeaning. It is protection. In short, the Church recognizes that women do not have the base of power that men have. The Bible uses terms like the "weaker partner" when referring to wives.[3] In another section the Bible instructs the Church to make sure that the needs of the older widows are met.[4] It says nothing about taking care of older widowers. Scripture strongly teaches that men have the primary obligation to provide for their families and brands anyone who does not do so as "worse than an unbeliever!"[5]

Another gift God gives to women is a sense of structure. Again, this idea is very unpopular among some people today, but it is very difficult to get around if we are going to be true to the teaching of Scripture. The structure, which is set in motion by marriage, is one of male headship: "For the husband is the head of the wife as Christ is the head of the church.... Now as the church submits to Christ, so also wives should submit to their husbands in everything."[6] This structure is based on mutual submission which should prevent a husband from trying to "lord it over" his wife.[7] The husband, although the head of the family, is to submit to his wife and to love her as Jesus loves the Church.[8] For the love of his wife, a man is to sacrifice himself as Christ sacrificed for the Church. When men keep these instructions in mind, marriage resembles an egalitarian (or equal) kind of relationship far more than a dictatorship. The husband rarely, if ever, needs to exert his authority over his wife. When there is a decision to be made and husband and wife disagree, the husband is given authority by God to direct the family. The husband is to be under Christ's authority. This provides structure for resolving differences. This structure for marriage is perfect when a couple is perfectly obedient to Christ. Since most people are not perfect in obedience however, most marriages are not perfect. But where couples try to obey Bible teaching, marriage will be characterized by mutual submission, that is, giving up self-will and going along with the other person's ideas. This kind of relationship is a beautiful gift.

While the Lord gives many things to women who follow Him, He also requires things from them. Just as there are Bible passages that instruct men to provide for their families and treat their wives in a loving way, there are also instructions for women—and some of them seem quite harsh on the surface. Many of these instructions have to do with women's roles in the family and the Church.

74 THE CHURCH

When Paul wrote to Timothy about the function of women in church meetings he mentioned some things that have puzzled, confused, and even angered people for centuries. Paul wrote, "I also want women to dress modestly, with decency and propriety, not with braided hair or gold or pearls or expensive clothes, but with good deeds, appropriate for women who profess to worship God.

"A woman should learn in quietness and full submission. I do not permit a woman to teach or to have authority over a man; she must be silent. For Adam was formed first, then Eve. And Adam was not the one deceived; it was the woman who was deceived and became a sinner. But women will be saved through childbearing—if they continue in faith, love and holiness with propriety."[9]

Wow! Sounds like Paul took a real broadside blast at women. On the first reading it would seem that the Bible is indicating that women should be wandering around pregnant and silent in plain-wrap clothing. Let's take this passage apart and see if this is what the Bible is teaching.

When reading any passage of Scripture it is important to compare it with other passages on the same subject. This gives a balanced view and helps to give a context to the idea as a whole.

When Paul wrote that women should not be overly adorned he was not writing so much about what a Christian is forbidden to wear as he is emphasizing where a Christian woman should be putting her efforts.

Peter takes up the same theme saying, "Your beauty should not come from outward adornment, such as braided hair and the wearing of gold jewelry and fine clothes. Instead, it should be that of your inner self, the unfading beauty of a gentle and quiet spirit, which is of great worth in God's sight."[10]

WOMEN IN THE CHURCH 75

The central point both Paul and Peter were trying to make was that God wants beauty to be something that comes from the inside. The issue is not hairstyle or jewelry. The issue is to be sure that more time and energy is spent working on the person behind the looks.

Some Christians have made a big deal about not wearing gold or expensive jewels based on these verses. These people misunderstand what Paul and Peter are trying to get across. While there may be a point at which it is wrong for a Christian woman to drape her body in excess of gold and jewels, the reason it is wrong is likely to have more to do with bad stewardship of the money God has given her than it has to do with overemphasizing her looks.

Paul riles up feminists with his statements instructing women to be submissive. I wish that there was an easy way to get around this idea but I'm afraid there is not one. The Bible does teach submission. It teaches that we all must be submissive to the governing authorities (which at the time this idea was penned were not very fair to people).[11] It teaches that children must submit to parents' authority.[12] It teaches that church members must submit to church leaders.[13] It teaches that slaves must submit to their masters even if they are harsh.[14] (However the early believers did everything they could to discourage slavery and there are historical accounts of congregations collecting funds to buy the freedom of slaves.) And of course, it teaches that we must submit above all to God.[15]

Christianity is a submissive religion. It is a belief system that requires us to be continually trying to give up pleasing ourselves while at the same time to be trying to make another person feel more loved and important.

If you are a die-hard feminist, or a die-hard any other

76 THE CHURCH

kind of "ist," you may have a very hard time with Christianity. Christianity requires that you quit "grinding your axe" and submit. Submit to your husband (or wife), to the Church, to your friends.

Naturally the Bible tells us that there is a point at which we must resist as well. If we are asked to violate one of God's principles we must resist. If we are asked to support something evil or immoral we must resist—even to death. It is this odd kind of submission and resistance that so puzzled the Roman government in their dealings with early Christians. The Romans could not figure out why these Christians would willingly submit to exhausting labor and unfair, humiliating restrictions but would resist to the death something as simple and easy to perform as burning a little incense in worship of Caeser. Both behaviors were acts of obedience and submission to the will of the Lord.

The thing we must keep in mind when thinking about submission is that all of us, men and women alike must be trying to make God the "boss." When we obey God by submitting to the authorities He has placed over us, we are really submitting to God. This example may be more clear-cut than are biblical instructions on church order.

In giving instructions for orderly worship, Paul made a point of noting that he did not allow women to teach or have authority over men. He required women to learn in "quietness and full submission." We have no way of knowing Paul's reasons for stating this rule. It may have something to do with the particular church he was writing to at the time (the church at Ephesus). It may have been directed at women who were not properly instructed and who were zealously misusing the new freedom they had found among the believers. It may have been that Paul was simply stating his own practice and was not issuing a standard for all churches. Or it may be that for all time women are not to teach at church gatherings.

Where then, can a woman serve in the Church? God has raised up women to help run churches, start Christian businesses, teach in Bible colleges, and travel as missionaries and evangelists. Christians must carefully consider their basis before claiming that these women were not chosen and gifted by God for such tasks.[16]

But many women who seek leadership roles in their churches still find a great deal of resistance from both men and women. Many people are not comfortable seeing women work in areas generally reserved for men. Others do not mind women holding certain positions, such as deacon, but feel the pastor should be a man. That just may have been the reason that Eileen had trouble starting her church. Of course if God is moving to start the neighborhood church, then all those disadvantages are just temporary annoyances which will someday evaporate like the morning mist.

DISCUSSION QUESTIONS

What, if anything, confuses you about women's roles in the Church? What steps can you take to help resolve your confusion?

**How does a relationship of mutual submission between men and women affect the process by which members of the Church come to conclusions on difficult issues such as the role of women?
In the Church all people have equal value but dif-**

78 THE CHURCH

ferent people have different levels of responsibility. Does this affect the way you view women's roles in the Church? Why or why not?

How has the content of this chapter influenced the way you see yourself serving the Church in the future?

NOTES
1. 1 Timothy 3:2
2. Galatians 3:28
3. 1 Peter 3:7
4. 1 Timothy 5:3
5. 1 Timothy 5:8
6. Ephesians 5:23,24
7. Matthew 20:25,26
8. Ephesians 5:21,25
9. 1 Timothy 2:9-15
10. 1 Peter 3:3
11. Romans 13:1-7
12. Ephesians 6:1
13. Hebrews 13:17
14. 1 Peter 2:18
15. James 4:7
16. 1 Corinthians 12:11

SEVEN
DON'T LOOK DOWN ON YOUTH

Don't let anyone look down on you because you are young, but set an example for the believers in speech, in life, in love, in faith and in purity. 1 Timothy 4:12

Some Bible scholars think that Timothy was about 30 years old when Paul wrote 1 Timothy. But in the first century, 30 was considered quite young for a leader in the Church. Paul's statement "Don't let anyone look down on you because you are young," leads us to believe that Timothy's youth was causing him some difficulties.

When Paul wrote those words he was really affirming not only Timothy but also anyone who is a part of the Church and happens to be young.

Jesus himself picked a youngster to be one of his closest disciples. John was probably in his teens when Jesus asked him to give up a future in the fishing industry and follow Him.[1]

But even though Jesus and Paul affirmed young people by both their words and their actions, many kids feel that they just "don't get no respect" from adults. They often are right. Many adults don't respect young people. They feel that although all people have equal value, respect must be earned. In fact, many adults don't respect other adults for the same reason.

So how can young people earn respect? Paul gave Timothy very sound advice when he said "Set an example

... in speech, in life, in love, in faith and in purity."[2] A young person who demonstrates these qualities would be considered mature and would be respected by most adults.

Young Christians have many opportunities to gain respect and show Christ's love to others by being examples for other members of their youth groups and for people within or outside of the church family. The effects of their attitudes and actions can be greater than they realize.

Terri Dawson was a visitor at First Church. She was brought on that crisp November morning by an aunt who was concerned for her spiritual welfare.

Both of Terri's parents were alcoholics. (Her dad was in far worse condition than her mom.) The additional responsibilities that her parents' problem created for Terri kept her out of many of the sports and leadership activities at school. She seemed to be a loner, although she truly wasn't. She was simply tired and burdened by shame.

Terri did not come from a Christian home. She did not own a Bible, and knew nothing of what faith in Christ meant.

Her aunt had recently become a Christian and was enthusiastic about getting her family to commit their lives to Christ. Most of them waved aside her invitations to attend church. But Terri was curious. She had noticed a considerable change in her aunt's life. Her interest whetted, Terri agreed to go to church with her aunt.

As Terri walked nervously up the sidewalk that led to the Christian Education building she noticed several kids she had seen before at school. They stared at her for a moment, but did not acknowledge her presence.

A round-shaped little lady pointed the way to the high school room and Terri nervously climbed the stairs and walked into the classroom marked "High School Grades 9-10."

Several students were in the room and were talking among themselves. Their conversation lagged a bit when they noticed Terri, but none of them greeted her.

Feeling alone and out of place, Terri began to wish that she had not come. Suddenly a tall woman walked into the class, her arms loaded down with papers and a huge Bible. She spoke to Terri immediately. "Hi, I'm Mrs. Bateman," said the woman. "I'm teaching this class, but I don't think I know you."

Terri briefly introduced herself and then settled in the rear of the class.

During the hour Terri spent with the high school group she experienced the warm embarrassment of being introduced by the teacher. She could feel herself being appraised by many of the students in the class. She also experienced the humiliation of not being able to find a passage of Scripture and of stumbling over the awkward names of Bible people and places as she read aloud. The pressure and fear of being expected to pray aloud in a small group made her even more uncomfortable.

Not once did any member of the youth group make more than a passing attempt to talk to Terri. No one invited her back to class or to any of the activities that were announced that morning.

Terri was not treated rudely intentionally. The members of the youth group simply were not caring enough to notice her. She was pretty much left alone in her uneasiness. If she wanted to be a part of this youth group she would need to be the one to put forth all of the effort.

A half mile away Stu was also experiencing his first visit to a church.

Stu had moved to the area from a rough and tumble section of the Texas panhandle. His twangy accent always brought a laugh in this part of the country, so he had learned to keep his mouth shut in the few weeks he and his mom had lived in town.

David had invited Stu to church. He also drove by that Sunday morning and picked Stu up.

When Stu arrived on the church grounds he already had a friend. David made a point of dragging Stu to every cluster of students, eagerly introducing him. (Stu would blush brightly every time.) At every introduction hands would be extended and names exchanged. There was a genuineness about the interest of these students that Stu could feel.

During class time members of the youth group fought good-naturedly about who would get to have Stu as part of their small group. One kid, a tall, lean fellow named Josh, found a Bible for Stu and explained how to use the table of contents. David nudged Stu and told him not to worry about being forced to participate. "New guys don't have to do anything that will make 'em feel dumb," he said reassuringly.

After class both teachers and students pumped Stu's hand and enthusiastically invited him to attend an upcoming camping trip.

Several days later Stu received a handwritten note from the teacher thanking him for attending the class and inviting him back. And back he went.

The contrast between Stu's and Terri's experiences is obvious. In both cases the obligation to act in a way that honors Christ is the responsibility of the youth group. Their response to this obligation can turn a person towards Christ or away from Him.

All youth groups have a great responsibility. They must take this responsibility very seriously for they will be accountable to God for their actions.

A quick test of how a youth group is doing is to ask this question: "Who or what is the focal point of this group?" If the answer is "Jesus," the group gets an *A*.

The youth group that is centered on the Lord will grow and mature in ways that please Him. Such groups usually have in common other characteristics that help them to be effective ministries.

Effective Youth Ministries Express Friendship and Love to Others

Cliques and the old "My group is cooler than your group" attitudes have no place among Christian youth. While cliques may be accepted social organizations at high school, they should not be "in" with believers whether on the campus or at church.

Sadly this is not always the case. Some youth groups are very unchristian towards outsiders, especially if the outsider is quite different or is a threat to the pecking order that the group has established by being just a little better looking, more talented, or more interesting than most. Those whose little youth group society may be affected go into action to freeze out the invader.

The example of what happened to Terri is tragically typical of many youth groups. It is very odd behavior for those who claim to know Christ. But as important as being loving and friendly is, it is not the only essential ingredient for a vital, well-respected group.

Youth Groups Need to Be Responsible
If you have ever helped clean up after a party you may have noticed the lack of regard that some people show for the property and labor of others. You may have found cookies ground into the carpet, punch spilled down the cabinets, or gum stuck to the furniture.

This shouldn't happen among Christians—particularly among members of the youth group. Cleaning up messes, having regard for the property of others, and looking to ease the burden of the other people in the church should be distinctives of every youth group. (Of course far too often it is the kids who go home and the adults who are left to clean up the mess.)

Youth Groups Know How to Have Fun!
There is still a lot of little kid left in the average sixteen-year-old. Big kids still want to go out and play—of course not with the same things that little children play with, but in a more sophisticated way. Part of the job of any youth group is to encourage good clean fun.

Fun is not "unspiritual." The Bible is full of examples of celebrations.[3] Christians should rejoice in life since they know the One who created all the enjoyable things in the first place.

Society seems to give many people the idea that fun is getting loaded on drugs or alcohol or that it is having a string of sexual conquests. These actions reflect more of a thrill of rebellion than an enjoyment of pure fun. These actions and attitudes do not honor Christ. They are ultimately destructive.

There are few things more destructive to a youth group than having a large portion of its members leading dual lives, trying to fit in with unbelievers at school or while out partying and playing the Christian kid at church meetings. This double life simply doesn't work. No one in the youth group is fooled for long and it certainly is a crummy example of what Christianity is all about for any younger or non-Christian kids who may be watching. Any youth group is dead in the water if a substantial number of its members are trying to play both sides of the fence.

Youth Groups Need to Be Loyal
In an average town there are plenty of things going on in various churches that can be of interest: a concert, a special speaker, some cute members of the opposite sex. But a local church can only function properly if its members are loyal, not spiritual butterflies floating around from group to group drinking the nectar without settling down and getting involved. While there is nothing wrong with enjoying fellowship with other believers in other churches, it should not be done at the expense of the fellowship we call our own.

Youth Groups Need to Be Involved
We live in a spectator culture. Most people sit back and watch things happen rather than participate. Involvement is not popular.

The members of a youth group need to be willing to get their hands dirty. They need to be involved in the planning, running, and cleaning up of youth events. They need to contribute.

Kids can help with mail outs, calling, photography, art, speaking, setting up or taking down and hundreds of other things that make the youth group an involvement experience and not just entertainment.

Youth Groups Need Commitment

The events and activities of the church body must have a high priority in order for a youth group to be successful. Jobs, sports, and other activities should be built around regular church events where possible rather than put before it. This is good training in godly living.

So friendship, love, responsibility, fun, loyalty, and involvement are all essential ingredients of a vital youth group. But how does the youth group fit in with its sponsoring church?

As with many of the things that we think of as natural parts of the church, the idea of a youth group is not found in the Bible and there is no evidence that early believers had anything vaguely similar. This may seem strange since a strong youth group is now thought of as one of the most important components of a church. In fact, many parents will choose to attend a church because it has a good youth program for their kids.

The Bible never mentions Sunday School, camp, or many of the other things that we have come to think of as part of the Church. But this does not mean that those things are wrong to do. (It does mean that is perfectly alright to have a church that functions without them.)

Most things such as Sunday School and youth groups are very new additions to church life. The Sunday School tradition is a little more than 100 years old and it may surprise you to know that it was not until the seventies that most churches felt it was important to have a youth pastor on their staffs.

Of course there were plenty of teenagers around before the sixties and seventies. But what caused a need for youth ministries were changes in society. Special ministries developed to meet the needs of young people in a changing world.

Since then, what has in effect happened is that many churches have created two congregations: one of older folks and the other of kids. While this may please both adults and kids alike, in the long run it may not be best for the church as a whole.

Youth and old age both bring important elements to the Church. Youth brings energy, idealism, vitality, and a robust joy for living and discovery. But youth can also display foolishness, recklessness, naiveté, shortsightedness, and gross inexperience!

Old age brings with it a wealth of wisdom, experience, realism, and healthy caution. But older people often lack the important attitudes of excitement, optimism, and sense of wonderment that young people offer.

In short both the young and the old need each other more than they realize. They balance each other so that one does not tip the scales in a burst of excessive exuberance and the other does not get weighed down by being overly cautious and stale. It is not healthy for a youth group to be so separated from the rest of the church body that they forget they are just one part of a whole group of people who are all trying to become like Christ.

Some youth groups go out of their way to show the rest of the church that they care about them. Recently at a youth group planning meeting those attending decided to select one adult church member each month to whom they could show special love and appreciation. The first person selected was the church custodian (often the most unsung servant of the Lord). The youth group managed to get into the church building one night before the custodian arrived to do his regular pre-Sunday cleanup. Like the legendary elves in the shoemaker shop they worked wonders on the whole facility.

As they left, a card was hung up and signed by all the members of the group. The card told the custodian how much they appreciated his work. A box of homemade cookies was left with it.

The following month the raiders of love hit the home of an elderly shut-in. They mowed the lawn, fixed screens, and cleaned the whole house. They sat down and talked to the fragile grandma who was the recipient of their kindness. She wept with appreciation and joy at the love shown to her by these young members of the Body of Christ.

It is actions like these that make a difference in how we are thought of by the rest of the church. It is actions like these that make the younger years of our lives rich.

DISCUSSION QUESTIONS

Think of a time when you felt you were at a disadvantage because you were young. How did you react towards those around you?

In what ways might gaining the respect of the adults in your church affect the way they respond to you?

What are some steps you can take to try to earn the respect of the adults in your life? How might

your example affect these adults? Other kids your age?

How might you feel if you were not receiving the respect you were trying to earn? What further steps could you take?

NOTES
1. Mark 1:19,20
2. 1 Timothy 4:12
3. 1 Kings 8:65,66; 1 Chronicles 15:16

EIGHT

ROTTEN APPLES IN THE BARREL

Command certain men not to teach false doctrines any longer . . . . The goal of this command is love, which comes from a pure heart and a good conscience and a sincere faith. Some have wandered away from these and turned to meaningless talk.
1 Timothy 1:3,5,6

Men, women and children stood patiently in line waiting to receive their cup of Kool Aid. It could have been the punch and cookie line at any church potluck. The people represented a variety of ages, races, and economic and educational backgrounds. But this was not any normal refreshment line. This line led to the greatest tragedy of its kind on record.

The first participants took their beverages, drinking them down on the spot. Then they helped the small children with theirs.

Within minutes the stomach cramps started. Soon the pain escalated to the point where the victims doubled over and began to moan in misery. Little children began to cry and shriek. Parents tried to comfort them, but were soon lost in their own suffering.

The other members of the congregation did nothing. They merely stood impassively in line waiting for their Kool Aid.

The place was a compound in the jungles of Guyana called Jonestown. The date was November 18, 1978. On that day 913 people died by cyanide poisoning. A few were murdered as they tried to escape. But for the vast majority it was suicide—the largest mass suicide in history.

Jim Jones, a former Christian pastor, stood on the deck of his jungle home. He watched the dying hundreds writhe in agony. He surveyed the field of corpses. It was he who had ordered his followers to drink cyanide-laced punch. It was he who had moved his flock from California to the jungles of Guyana. The move helped Jones avoid the government harassment over his increasingly bizarre treatment of his followers—members of the People's Temple.

It was Jones who ordered the murders of a fact-finding group who came to the jungle village to investigate accusations that members of the church were being abused. (Several newsmen and a United States congressman were killed.)

Now Jim Jones pulled a revolver from his hip holster. He pressed the barrel against his head, stiffened his grip, and squeezed sharply on the trigger. Jones' death was instant and violent.

Several days later when the first camera crews flying over Jonestown with helicopters beamed back video shots of the bloated blackened corpses strewn about the compound, the world was shocked and stunned. "How could this happen?" people asked. Suddenly all sorts of faces appeared on the television screen talking about the weird antics and danger signs of the People's Temple. Of course in hindsight it is always easier to say, "I knew something wasn't right about those guys!"

Jim Jones was a false teacher. He distorted, bullied, brainwashed, and abused. But he also offered the people who followed him to South America something that they needed and were not getting anywhere else. Jones provided security, direction, and his own brand of sympathy and compassion. He was a liar and a deceiver, but he was a talented liar. Many people allowed their children and themselves to be slaughtered for his "truth."

Most false teachers do not take such a drastic turn as did Jim Jones. Many of them are smooth and easy to take. In fact, many of them are quite good at using bits of truth and Christian language in their schemes to honor themselves or to make a buck.

Great loads of genuine believers fall prey to the antics of the rotten apples who have wormed their way to the top of the pile. If these believers are lucky, they will be relieved of just some money and a bit of their pride as a result of getting mixed up with a phony. The more unfortunate may become victimized, confused, and eventually disillusioned with or bitter about Christianity itself.

False teachers often fall into one of two groups: (1) those who are off-track in their thinking, who spread their untrue ideas and (2) those who teach biblical information but are frauds personally such as TV preachers who are in the business for financial gain.[1] Those who are off in their thinking are not people who have disagreements over minor issues; many Christians differ on such things as order of worship, dress, and church organization. There is room in the Church for such differences. But false teachers differ on what are called "salvation issues." They may not believe that Jesus is God's only Son or that His death on the cross paid the penalty for our sins. These beliefs are essential for all Christians.

People who claim to be Christian but who oppose Christian teaching on salvation issues are called *heretics*. People who once believed in Jesus as Savior but who fall away from their belief are called *apostates*. And those who claim to be righteous Christians but whose life-style is far from the principles taught in the Bible are called *hypocrites*.

Some of these bad apples make their way around the country as traveling ministers. Others work within a local congregation spreading disharmony like a cancer.

A Southern California TV preacher who recently saw his empire topple is a good example of a phony imitating spirituality for personal gain. Pretending to be in direct communication with God, this evangelist and faith healer prowled the stage declaring "prophesies" (most of them spin-offs of biblical teachings). As a part of his show and "ministry" he would venture into the audience pretending that the voice of God was directing him to certain individuals: "There is a man from Tyler, Texas—who is suffering from a ruptured disc." The evangelist would ask for the person described in such "prophetic" statements to identify himself. The poor sufferer, astonished that this total stranger would know so much about him and his ailment, would often burst into tears as he rose to his feet to receive the "healing" that was promised by the TV preacher. The audience was impressed and the people in TV-land were impressed. They sent their cards and letters and their five dollar bills. The TV preacher turned into a fat cat.

But some observers smelled a rat. The act was too slick, the performance, too polished and precise. It seemed more like a magic trick than an act of God. In fact it was a professional magician who knew the tricks of the trade who exposed the faith healer to the world.

The magician did not believe God was helping this TV preacher pinpoint which strangers in his congregation had which specific ailments. He thought the whole act was a hoax.

The magician sat in the back of the hall during a taping of a healing service. In his pocket was a small radio receiver and a tape deck. On his head he wore a headset which enabled him to hear radio transmissions. As the evangelist wove his way through the anxious flock, the magician could distinctly hear the voice of a woman slowly announcing the name of an individual, his location in the room, and his clothes, hometown, and specific illness. As she spoke the evangelist would make his way through the auditorium and feigning a revelation from heaven, would find his target, and fire his pitch.

It turned out that the preacher had a small radio receiver in his ear. The voice from heaven was really the voice of an accomplice reading information that she had gathered while circulating through the crowd before the start of the meeting. The man and his act were both phonies. He was a false teacher masquerading as one whose desire was to do good for others. He was a wolf, a parasite, an imposter, falsely representing himself to the world as a Christian healer and ultimately discrediting the name of Jesus.

False teachers make the news when they go way off the deep end. But they have been among believers, like sharks circling the Christian community, since the beginning of the Church.

Jesus warned of them. Paul described them and even named names in his letter to Timothy.[2] Yet false teachers continue to plague Christians, especially the young in understanding, the gullible, or those who stray too far from the protection of the Church.

Not all false teachers end up serving poison punch in the jungle. In fact, most of the false teachers throughout history closely resembled Christians. But they are made

ROTTEN APPLES IN THE BARREL 97

of different stuff; they are not the genuine article.

One of the trademarks of a false religion is that it generally has a leader who claims he is in cahoots with God. This special relationship is copied from genuine Christianity in which people like Moses, Nathan, Elisha, and even the apostles were recognized as having authority from God. (Jesus cannot be placed on that list because He *is* God.)

A modern and familiar example of false teaching that tries hard to pass itself off as the genuine article is Mormonism (or as they are officially known The Church of Jesus Christ of Latter-Day Saints).

You may have friends who are Mormons or may know kids from school who belong to this cult. They do not seem particularly weird or bizarre. They hardly seem like the kind who would swallow poison because their church told them to. Nor do they seem completely off base. They use many of the same words as Christians and they claim to believe the Bible. For the most part they are clean, wholesome, sincere, all-American types. Just like a certain kind of bad apple, nice and polished on the outside but a bit wormy on the inside, the Mormon church has established itself as a nice alternative to Christianity. But Mormons are not Christians (although it may be possible to find some genuine albeit mixed up Christians in their midsts). The leaders and people of Mormonism are very, very sincere. But sincerity is never an indication of genuine truth. They are sincerely wrong.

The Mormon view of God, the Bible, Jesus and a great many other things varies widely from what Christians have always believed. Like most other false religions they have a key human (the president or prophet of the church) who gets direct messages from God that everyone in the cult is to follow. In their short history, they have had God tell them to practice polygamy (having more than one wife), to forbid polygamy, to add books to Scripture, to not allow blacks the rite of priesthood (an important rite for all Mormon men) and then not to forbid blacks from holding the priesthood. The god of the Mormons changes his mind when under social pressure to do so.

Like many other false religions, Mormonism offers some attractive enticements. They are a tight, family-oriented group. They take care of their own people and offer comradeship and warmth to those who come into their midst hurting. Few suspect that they are being led into a maze of beliefs that stunts their understanding and spiritual growth.

It is an assumption of Scripture that the secular world is full of false teachers. One needs only to tune into TV or radio for a few moments to hear the hype of their false messages. "Grab all the gusto you can," one ad urges. Me-first materialism drips from the speakers. Ideas that suggest the universe can get along without the involvement of God, or that stress the importance of fame, money, power, looks, and man's own accomplishments are the common fare of the world. These are clearly unbiblical, false teachings, dangerous distractions. Like the orchestra on the *Titanic*, worldly false teachers may make a lot of nice noise but they sink with the ship.

Every Christian needs to know how to spot false teaching or to put it another way, how to avoid being a sucker.

The first step is to avoid being a people follower. This may be a bit harder than you imagine. Most of us get a thrill out of seeing a movie star or a rock artist (this is true even in Christian music circles). Most of us have a favorite performer, writer, speaker, or musician whom we admire and listen to. In a way, our admiration gives these celebrities authority—whether they deserve it or not.

Of course the slicker and more articulate a speaker is, the more easily we find what they say to be believable. If it goes contrary to good sense we may question our own beliefs in view of the wisdom of this "authority."

The desire to be taught by someone who knows what he or she is talking about is deeply ingrained in humans. But that authority needs to be given to the only one who can teach us truthfully—Jesus Christ.

So the first step is that we must become less enamored with people. We must become less dependent upon being told what to believe or to do and become determined to follow directly the teachings of the Bible.

This is not such an easy task in a world where the media blitzes us with the new heroes and leaders of the moment. We are constantly being presented with someone new to hear from, learn from, or honor. Added to this is the fact that many people like the security of knowing that there is someone out there whom they can trust, someone to whom God speaks, someone they can look up to as a role model, someone who is a hero of the faith.

But people always disappoint us. Our leaders have feet of clay and oftentimes very faulty vision. A careful study of many of the popular figures in recent Christian history can show that true men of God often muddled some of their ideas or behavior. To put our trust in people rather than God and His Word is to be asking for disappointment.

The second step is to really know what it is that you as a Christian believe, not just a creed or quickly rattled-off verses, but a well-thought-out stand. Just as important is to know *why* we believe. If our faith is based on that of our parents, or on blind emotionalism, we are on very dangerous ground.

Many cults base their teachings on a felt experience rather than solid biblical truth. Truth based on feeling can vary from mood to mood. It may depend far more on what we had for dinner last night than on what God has to say to us.

Truth can stand investigation, but an experience cannot be investigated or tested. One must simply believe the word of the person describing the experience or reject it. (Note: Christianity does have an experiential element in it but these feelings and experiences will never be contrary to the teachings of Scripture.) Some Christians point to their own experiences as proof of God's truth. But experience alone is a shaky basis for belief. Some followers of the New Age Movement claim that they get power from crystals. A person cannot discredit their experiences without calling the people involved either liars or crazy. The fact that Christianity is true and The New Age Movement is false does not prove or disprove these experiences.

There are many books that can explain the reasons for being a Christian. These arguments in defense of the truth and divine origin of Christianity form a branch of theology called apologetics. Books on apologetics may be difficult to read and technical or elegant in their simplicity such as C.S. Lewis's *Mere Christianity*. They can be found in or ordered from most Christian bookstores and can help you stand firm in your faith. As the old saying goes "You must stand for something or you will fall for anything." Hopefully what you decide to take a stand for will not crack and crumble under close scrutiny or criticism.

One of the reasons why some Christians are so unprepared to ward off faulty thinking is that they spend so little time in study of the Scriptures. Almost everything else comes first: school, friends, sports, TV. The time left to check out God's Word is short or nonexistent. During the week most Bibles remain unopened and unmoved. It is small wonder that some Christians are such easy prey for the inviting cults or strange teachings.

False teachers launch their attacks at the core of Christian beliefs: the divinity of Jesus and His saving death and resurrection. Cults are able to sweep up so many followers because so many of those who call themselves Christians are illiterate about their faith. The greatest danger posed by false teachers does not lie in how bizarre they appear to be, but in their close resemblance to Christianity. They seem to be genuine, so they fool the gullible and those who have not taken the time to examine closely the ideas and true teachings of Jesus.

In the end, God will sort out those who have intentionally spun or passed on lies and those who were merely caught in the web. He will be gracious or severe according to His own criteria. But for those of us who can, it is better to know enough not to get caught in the first place.

DISCUSSION QUESTIONS

What dangers are associated with becoming involved in a false religion or believing a false teaching?

What standards can you use to evaluate if someone is a false teacher? If you don't know, where will you go for help?

102 THE CHURCH

What do you as a Christian believe is true about God, Jesus, and the Bible? Why do you believe these things are true? What steps can you take to help you be able to express clearly what you believe?

How can you express your concern to someone who is being influenced by the ideas of false teachers? Why is it important for you to share your concern with that person?

NOTES
1. 1 Timothy 6:3-5
2. 1 Timothy 1:18-20

NINE

SHIP-WRECKED FAITH

Fight the good fight, holding on to faith and a good conscience. Some have rejected these and so have shipwrecked their faith.
1 Timothy 1:18,19

You can see them everywhere. Their pictures are broadcast on the evening news, published in the daily newspaper. You can read all about them in the *Enquirer* or take a good long look at some of them in *Playboy*. They are Christians. Christians who have made a real mess of their lives. They are self-destructing publicly, cremating their reputations. And since there is nothing like a good scandal to sell papers and magazines, the media fans the ashes of their lives as long as they can hope for one more quick burst of flame. These Christians have shipwrecked their faith.

The Church is made up of not only those who for the most part have succeeded in living the Christian life, but also those who have failed to be faithful to the Lord. No Christian is perfect. In fact the apostle John said, "If we claim to be without sin, we deceive ourselves and the truth is not in us."[1] But later in the same letter John said, "Whoever claims to live in him must walk as Jesus did."[2] Christians must realize that none of us is without sin, but we must also try to walk in Jesus' steps. Sometimes our attempts fail. We get off course. But there is a great deal of difference between being shipwrecked and being off course.

At one time or another every Christian falls short of the high standards God has set for us. Each of us fail, we open our mouths before engaging our minds, or act before thinking about the correctness and consequences of our actions. Each of us has failed at times to listen to the Holy Spirit nudging our conscience. The remedy to these departures from the path God has set for us is to confess our wrongdoings to God and to get back on track.[3]

To shipwreck or crash our faith into the rocks is quite another thing. The apostle Paul warned Timothy that ignoring the guidance of conscience would lead to "shipwrecked faith." Apparently two men in the early church had fallen into sin and false doctrine. It seems these men were not sorry for their actions and were continuing in their sinful ways. Paul described their faith as "shipwrecked."[4]

The picture a shipwreck paints in our minds is one of a damaged vessel broken up in a raging sea. A shipwreck usually causes pain or loss of life. It may hurt innocent victims.

The things that shipwreck faith may be acts of sexual immorality but can also be acts of greed, theft, pride—well, the list could go on and on. A person can end up with shipwrecked faith if he or she allows some area to get out of control and then refuses to repent and straighten things out. A term for this kind of behavior is "habitual sin." John is one person I knew who fell to it.

John was a youth worker in a large church. He was sharp and energetic. The kids all liked him and the adults were pleased with the job he was doing.

Because John was single, he had a tremendous amount of time to devote to working with students. His charming personality made his job easier and more enjoyable.

John recruited a core group of high school students to serve as leaders in the youth group. These were the kids whom John felt had both spiritual maturity and natural leadership qualities. He spent a lot of time developing especially strong relationships with these student leaders.

John had almost every area of his life firmly under control. He was not a flake. But like most of us, he did have one spot where the ice was particularly thin: John had trouble controlling his sexual urges. Until now, he had managed to avoid any problems in this area by the sheer amount of work he was trying to do. His busyness kept him out of trouble.

The core group changed all of that. For in that group he developed a particularly close relationship with Brenda, a high school junior.

Brenda had an enormous crush on John. She leaned on his shoulder in a way that suggested more than playfulness. She made eye contact with him whenever she could, blushing when he returned her gaze. She insisted on being the last to be dropped off when he drove kids home from church events.

John sensed Brenda's interest and found himself asking her to help him with various projects that didn't really need a second hand. John was drawing closer to Brenda than he was to any other kids in the youth group. Roughhousing with her was his form of seductive game playing.

It was not too long before John and Brenda had a full-blown affair raging in private. John was riddled with guilt and fear. He wanted to end the relationship but was afraid that Brenda would retaliate by "spilling the beans."

Everything that he had worked for in the church was in jeopardy. He yielded control to his sexual appetite time after time. His sexual liaison with Brenda was like a force that with increasing speed hurled him toward the rugged rocks of disaster.

Before too long the affair became obvious to the other students and soon the parents and the church staff were involved. John's ministry exploded into a million pieces. He, Brenda, and Brenda's parents left the church. John left youth work for good.

Sin is sin. This is simple and very true. God does not consider one sin as being less important than another. The Bible teaches that all of us have sinned, either by what we have done or what we haven't done.

But some sins obviously have heavier earthly consequences than others. For example swiping a candy bar and having sex before marriage are both considered sin by God. The consequence for swiping a candy bar may be nothing if you don't get caught. If you do get caught, it is unlikely that you will spend much time in jail. You may very well be humiliated by having your sin public and you may be grounded for life by your parents, but the consequences are not nearly as devastating as the scars premarital sex can create.

Suppose you go to bed with your prom date. You may not get caught in the act, but you may start a baby that you are unprepared to raise. Even if you use birth control, it fails a certain percentage of the time.

Condoms have a failure rate of 10 percent. Think about that the next time someone talks about "safe" sex. Would you play Russian roulette if the odds were upped from five to one to nine to one?

Sex can give you herpes—a gift that keeps on giving. One out of ten people have this nasty little virus. Many of them would be happy to pass it along. (As you probably know, herpes is an incurable venereal disease.)

Then of course you may just get the virus called HIV which causes AIDS. This will be one of the last consequences you suffer since the odds are very likely that you will die within a few years.

And even if you escape the physical risks of premarital sex you probably will suffer some psychological or emotional damage. Your future relationship with your spouse will be less than the best that God wants for you.

Clearly it is not advisable to be involved in either swiping candy or having premarital sex. But one can see that the consequences of each of these sins are very different.

Most people who commit sins figure that they will never get caught. They see themselves as invincible, lucky, or too smart. The world is full of broken people who thought their sins wouldn't catch up to them. But there are no exceptions to God's laws, just illustrations of it. It's just a matter of time.

Sin is sin. But some sins can be particularly devastating when people in positions of responsibility are involved. It is clearly sin to get mad at your boss and cuss him or her out. The probable consequence is losing your job. This may be an inconvenience if you are in high school and depend on your job to put gas in your tank and buy hamburgers at the golden arches. But it could be a disaster if you have a sick wife and three hungry kids to support at home. It is a tragedy when any person bails out on his or her family and runs off with a lover from the office. It is a disaster when that person is the leader of a Christian organization or the pastor of a church.

Obviously, the more recognition a person has the greater his or her responsibility to avoid sin of any kind, especially public sin. The higher the profile of a leader the greater the number of people who get damaged when the leader's life goes out of control and smacks a reef.

The Bible warns that not many of us should seek a position of high responsibility because teachers and other leaders "will be judged more strictly" if they blow it.[5] This warning can be applied to more than pastors, youth workers, and others in the local church. It can also apply to those who want to be writers, rock'n' roll stars, speakers, or TV preachers.

Each group of Christians has a responsibility to help prevent the shipwreck of those who fellowship with them. In fact Jesus gives very clear instructions for the Church to act on if they see one of their members seriously heading off course. This is called church discipline and it is not practiced too often anymore. It is a very important part of the responsibility that Jesus says Christians have to serve each other. Jesus means for church discipline to be practiced in every church that claims to believe in Him.

The idea behind church discipline is to correct the direction that a person is steering their life and to bring it back on course with the clear teaching of the Bible. Of course this is where it gets a little sticky. Not every church agrees with the others about all the teachings of Scripture. But we agree on enough to give guidance to 95 percent of the people who go off course.

Since the purpose is to restore a straying believer and not to just meddle in their affairs, a church must be very careful to get their facts straight and not to make issues out of non-issues. But they must also have some recourse to take if a person rejects their attempts to straighten them out and put them back on God's navigational plan.

The early church used something called "excommunication" as an ultimate threat to a believer. Basically excommunication means to kick a person out of fellowship

110 THE CHURCH

with other Christians. Excommunication may seem mean-spirited and it would be if all the steps that go before it are not considered. But the Bible teaches that this is the ultimate form of church discipline: to disown a renegade believer. Other Christians were told to have nothing to do with the person who has been excommunicated. The purpose of this action is to bring the wayward person to repentance.

For an example of how excommunication is to be used, let's take an actual case from the Bible.[6] We know the sin the person committed and enough of the steps that were taken to give us a good idea of how the discipline worked. I've filled in the blanks with my view of what probably took place.

Edgar Knucklehead Acropolopolis (er—he wasn't specifically named in Scripture so I took the liberty of making up his name) lived in the city of Corinth. Because of its importance as a trade center, Corinth was always boiling with a strange mix of foreign ideas. Each traveler to the city brought his own unusual belief and practices with him. The government in Rome was very tolerant of differing moral attitudes in different regions of the empire.

In first-century Corinth almost anything could happen. The residents of the city could have their pick of ideologies, sexual experiences, or gods.

The little home church had begun to grow and was drawing many from this sewer of sin to faith in a cleansing God. Edgar was a member of one of the little home churches. No one is really sure how the information leaked out, but it did. Edgar was sexually involved with an older woman—his mother!

Following the principles laid down by Christ[7] a member of the church went to Edgar privately and asked him if the information he had heard was true. When Edgar reluctantly admitted that it was accurate his friend from church told him in no uncertain terms that this behavior was sin and must cease. Edgar nodded in agreement. The friend offered his help and prayers. But Edgar seemed hesitant to take any assistance. "Edgar, are you going to cease from this kind of behavior and repent?" Edgar merely shrugged his shoulders.

Within a week or so news came that Edgar was up to his old practices again. This time there were several members of the church at his door, including the friend who had confronted Edgar first.

The little group lovingly pointed out from Scripture the problem with Edgar's actions[8] and the price that Christ had paid to clean him from any kind of sin.[9] But Edgar stuck to vague answers and a clear lack of commitment to change.

The actions of the church stalled here. They continued to allow Edgar to fellowship with them. Perhaps they lacked the confidence to take the final step.

It was at this time that the apostle Paul was notified of the situation with Edgar. Writing from another city Paul's fiery words flew like hot sparks at the leadership of the church. Paul was shocked that they would allow a person to stay in the fellowship of believers while actively commiting a sin that "does not occur even among pagans."[10] Paul demanded that the church act on Edgar's case. If Edgar did not repent, excommunicate him. Or in Paul's words: "hand this man over to Satan so that the sinful nature may be destroyed and his spirit saved on the day of the Lord."[11]

The church called Edgar on the carpet. He was asked to come before the elders. By this time it is very likely that Edgar balked. He no doubt knew what was going to

112 THE CHURCH

take place, and like many other self-willed believers after him, he may have abandoned the Church.

Edgar's defection would not keep the Church from doing its job. They officially excommunicated Edgar and asked their people to pray for him but only to extend their hand in fellowship if Edgar was truly willing to abandon his perverted sin. In all other respects they were told to treat him like they would an evil tax collector.

The little house church also put out the word on Edgar to all the other little house churches. He was ignored by the whole Christian community.

This may sound like odd behavior for Christians to practice. Shunning a person, booting him out of the fellowship of believers, hassling him numerous times. It may seem off, but it is the prescription the Bible give for treatment of those who will not submit themselves to "course correction" on their lives.

The action may have worked. Some Bible scholars believe that Paul briefly mentions in another letter to the church in Corinth the case of Edgar and his subsequent reinstatement as a member in good standing of the fellowship.[12]

So simply stated, the actions to take if you see a friend who claims to be a Christian getting way off course are:

1. *Go to him yourself.* Be humble and loving. Approach him about his problem. Ask him if he needs help and try to get it for him. (Some people may have problems bigger than you can handle by yourself.) Pray with him. Be clear in letting him know that what he is doing is wrong. Be prepared to show him where the Bible says that it is wrong. Let him know you care.

2. If the person does not stop his sin it is time to *get other people involved.* Go to one or two trustworthy Chris-

tians and share what you know and have done so far. Go as a team and repeat the actions in step one again.
3. If the person continues to sin, *involve the leadership of the church*. Call the believer on the carpet and lovingly tell him he can either repent or face expulsion from the group of believers.
4. If he does not turn his actions around *vote him out of the church* and let your congregation know that they are to pray for the person, but not to hang out with him except to try and help him.
5. If the person repents, take him back and love him just like nothing happened (just the way God does with us when we sin).

Some of you reading these words may have already rammed up on the rocks of life. Your Christian life is a mess. You may want to know, can a shipwreck be rebuilt? You bet! But it takes work.

First, get your relationship with God straightened out and stop doing anything that will further damage your faith.

You may have to make restitution (paying back a debt) or go to someone and ask for forgiveness. You may have to apologize to the church or to your youth group.

If you have let someone down, realize it may take time for that person to have a lot of trust in you. It is part of the price of rebuilding.

Find someone who will hold you accountable, someone who will watch out for you and advise you if they sense you are getting off course again.

Keep a close eye on your day-to-day relationship with God. It doesn't take too many days of being preoccupied with other things to forget about God and find ourselves

114 THE CHURCH

drifting perilously close to the reef-infested waters. If you already know what shipwrecked faith is like, you probably won't want to experience it twice.

DISCUSSION QUESTIONS

The apostle Paul wrote that rejection of faith and good conscience can lead to shipwrecked faith. Why do you suppose this is true?

If you were to shipwreck your faith, who would be affected?

What would you point to as some of the danger zones or "rocks" that could cause disaster to your faith? What can you do to identify and deal with these weak spots?

What must a Christian do in order to get back on course, or salvage a shipwrecked faith? Which of these things would be the hardest for you to do?

How should you respond to someone who has shipwrecked their faith?

NOTES
1. 1 John 1:8
2. 1 John 2:6
3. 1 John 2:1-3
4. 1 Timothy 1:18-20
5. James 3:1
6. 1 Corinthians 5:1-5
7. Matthew 18:15-17
8. Leviticus 18:8
9. Romans 6:6
10. 1 Corinthians 5:1
11. 1 Corinthians 5:5
12. 2 Corinthians 2:5-8

TEN

THE CHURCH AND THE "LEAST OF THESE"

> *"Then the righteous will answer him, 'Lord, when did we see you hungry and feed you, or thirsty and give you something to drink? When did we see you a stranger and invite you in, or needing clothes and clothe you? When did we see you sick or in prison and visit you?'*
>
> *"The King will reply, 'I tell you the truth, whatever you did for one of the least of these brothers of mine, you did for me.'"* Matthew 25:37-40

The helicopter hovered in the air a quarter of a mile above the ground. Seated uncomfortably on board were a camera crew, a field director, and a prominent television evangelist. The field director crouched in the cockpit, his voice hopelessly drowned out by the whirl of machinery overhead. He gestured wildly with his hands in the direction of a small field of rice surrounded by a few huts. The pilot moved the stick and the helicopter tipped in the direction indicated by the field director.

The purpose of this expedition was to show the folks back home in the USA the warm heart of the visiting evangelist. As part of his fund raising goals the preacher wanted to target some money for relief work. This brought him to the Philippines.

The moment his private jet landed in Manila he was met by the private limo of a rich government official. The evangelist was housed in the palatial splendor that comes with great wealth. His meals were sumptuous. His every need was taken care of by pampering servants. He spent most of the fact-finding week enjoying the many comforts offered by his host. When it came time to visit the needy for his documentary he was provided with a government helicopter and crew.

The little man working in the rice field could not help but notice the helicopter hovering in the sky above him. But his curiosity turned to bewilderment when the noisy bird dropped to the earth not more than 100 feet away.

The rice farmer wore nothing but a thin pair of shorts over his tanned body. Not yet fifty, his leathery body showed evidence of years in the tropical sun. The worn straw hat he wore cast shadows on the wrinkled etchings of his face. Clutching his hoe, his mouth gaped wide to show his toothless expression of shock. He was wind-whipped but stayed securely anchored to the silty floor of his rice paddy.

As the blades of the helicopter sputtered to a standstill the camera crew rolled out of the cramped quarters and began fiddling with their equipment. Then, with the assistance of the field director, a big-boned man stepped out of the door. He was dressed head to toe in a fashionable safari outfit. Crisp lines in the garments betrayed the fact that they had very recently been pressed. The evangelist walked to the edge of the rice paddy and surveyed the sight, he nodded in approval to the camera crew as they furiously wrestled with their equipment.

The field director began to call to the old man motioning him to come closer. The farmer, who until this moment had been pondering the events as he leaned on his staff, now waded hesitantly out of the rice paddy. The field director asked the farmer his name and informed him that he was to have the privilege of appearing on film with a traveling dignitary from America. The farmer seemed delighted at the idea and broke into an all-gum grin.

The cameramen gave the signal and the field director drew an X in the dirt for the farmer to stand upon. The evangelist was told that the old man's name was Benito. With this bit of necessary information the preacher went straight into his part like the professional showman he was.

"This is my dear friend Benito," he said pulling the man to his side with a Rolex-gilded arm. "Benito needs your help. He needs the gospel preached in his village. He needs help to provide the food and clothing his family must have to stay alive."

The poor farmer stared passively at the camera. The big evangelist squeezed the small man hard and his eyes narrowed and peered into the center of the lens, "Please send a thousand dollars, a hundred dollars, twenty dollars, but please, for Benito's sake—send something."

"Cut!" yelled the director. The evangelist dropped his grip on Benito and without saying a word walked back to the helicopter, brushing the dust of his encounter off of his pristine safari suit.

Within moments the camera crew and helicopter had disappeared leaving Benito standing alone in his field wondering if all this had just been a dream.

Within a few months the donations began pouring in to the evangelist's headquarters. The generosity of his television flock was motivated by the slick video piece featuring Benito. The safari-suited preacher had exchanged his "field wear" for a tailored suit and gold studded jewelry.

Benito worked the remaining years of his life on his little field. He never saw one penny of the money that was raised by using his picture. He never saw the video clip. In his mind the whole incident was an alien event that occurred one muggy afternoon. He never could figure out what it was all about.

Meanwhile in another community thousands of miles away the Church Planning Committee was meeting again. It had been six months since they had gotten the go-ahead from the congregation to proceed on plans for building the long overdue new sanctuary.

Quite clearly this new building would be the attraction of the neighborhood. The spiralling columns and the lavish fountains in the courtyard would give grace, beauty, and sophistication to the structure.

A famous architect had been retained and today's meeting would be the last review of the plans before construction began.

The planning committee members marveled at the small scale model of their new facility which had been brought by the architect. They were a bit taken back at the 20 thousand dollar price tag for the narthex stained glass windows, but were soothed as the architect described the meditative light that would twinkle through those pieces of colored glass.

Sure, they could have a much simpler building. Sure, they could have saved hundreds of thousands of bucks by going without the full pipe organ, the stained glass, the marble columns, the tile fountains, and the rest. But what kind of statement would that make to the neighborhood about the bountiful God they serve? How would a plain-wrapped church attract the wealthy believers in the area?

120 THE CHURCH

No, this would be a monument to God—a place of rest and beauty in a world of concrete and shopping malls.

As the meeting was about to begin, in a small cardboard hut just a two-hour drive away, a young Mexican mother wrapped her infant child in her shawl and placed her softly on an old mattress spread upon the dirt floor.

In a huge shopping mall Marie walked into a fashionable clothing store. She headed straight for the rack of jackets. Locating her size, she pulled a particularly attractive jacket off the hanger and slipped it on. Marie strolled to the full-length mirrors and admired the look of the jacket against her slim body. It was sleek and in high style right now. It also cost 200 dollars.

Marie debated with herself furiously for a moment. She did not need a new jacket. She had several that would be in fashion for another year or so. (If it was merely warmth she wanted her "old" jackets would be fine for many years to come.)

Two hundred dollars is a lot of money, she thought. She momentarily considered the fund raiser going on at her church—a bake sale to raise money for the homeless. *But even if I donated an amount equal to the price of this jacket it would do little to ease the suffering of those without a place to live,* she reasoned. *It takes big bucks—the kind governments or millionaires have to give to make any real difference. Besides, how would I know that the cash would go to help the poor and not just put gas in some administrator's BMW?*

Marie folded the jacket over her arm. She walked with it up to the counter. "Is this all for you, ma'am?" the clerk inquired. Marie nodded silently and opened her wallet.

THE CHURCH AND THE "LEAST OF THESE"

Something is wrong in the stories you've just read. Something in the behavior and thinking of each of these members of the Church is inconsistent with the teaching of their Lord.

One of the clear obligations of the Church is to consider and care for the poor. Tragically there are those who claim to be part of the Church who do nothing to help the poor. They may even actually exploit them further.

The clean-pressed TV evangelist in his safari suit cared nothing for the poor man in the field. He saw the farmer as a way to increase the donations given to him. The "man of God" enjoyed his expensive meals and being chauffeured back and forth between "performances." He treated his wife to diamonds from Tiffany and sent out engraved Christmas cards. The poor Philippino farmer saw no help from the funds raised by using his image.

The Church Planning Committee seemed to forget the primary mission of the Church. They were designing a country club when what their community needed was a lighthouse. They thought that ornamented surroundings would draw people to their church. They failed to realize that it should be the Holy Spirit magnetizing people with love that draws others into the Body regardless of whether or not the church grounds featured a tile fountain. Although they knew Jesus said, "Love your neighbor as yourself,"[1] they had also failed to see just who their neighbor was.

Marie failed to see that the Church is not just a big organization with lots of money and a core of wealthy, powerful men who do the contributing, but it is the individual members acting with care and responsibility. She did not see that her small sacrifice not only could help the needy, but it could help her soul.

The apostle Paul made an issue of the treatment of the penniless widows who were part of the Church. He wrote to Timothy telling him to instruct individual family members to bear the burden of the widow's support. If the widow was without family, the fellowship was to pick up the tab.[2]

While saying good-bye to the leaders of the church of Ephesus, Paul commented, "I have not coveted anyone's silver or gold or clothing. You yourselves know that these hands of mine have supplied my own needs and the needs of my companions. In everything I did, I showed you that by this kind of hard work we must help the weak, remembering the words and the Lord Jesus himself said: 'It is more blessed to give than to receive.'"[3] Christians are to share the money they earn with those who are weaker or who have less.

James commented, "Religion that God our Father accepts as pure and faultless is this: to look after orphans and widows in their distress and to keep oneself from being polluted by the world."[4] Caring for the needy is a pure and faultless way to serve the Lord.

Jesus Himself spoke many times on the obligation that believers have to use their wealth compassionately. In fact He went so far as to indicate that in showing practical love to someone in need we are really showing our love to Him.[5]

In a world made smaller every day by rapid transportation, electronic media, and print, it is getting harder and harder to excuse ourselves for not treating those across our borders or in another town as if they are neighbors. Their suffering becomes our shame—and to some degree our fault. We surround ourselves in abundance while our fellow believers lack the necessities of life.

Each group of believers, each church and individual in it, must wrestle with the hard questions of "How much is too much?" and "What is really important for me to have and what is not?"

Some churches have figured out the answers to these questions already.

The small congregation that meets on the dusty hillside in Tijuana uses all pre-owned furniture in their homes and church. Most do not own a car. They take public transportation or walk. Most of them wear second-hand clothing. Few own their own homes. None of them have boats, motorhomes, or a cabin on the lake. Only a handful have televisions. Many do not have electricity or gas in their homes. They cook over kerosene stoves. They live in ramshackled huts without running water or sewer. Most of them live with their families in a one-room house. They are fortunate to work all week and make $50. These are the people who make up the church in the Colonia Groupo. Yet as desperately poor as these people are themselves, they collect a few meager pesos each month and send them to support those who are living in even worse conditions.

By all rights the people in this church deserve to be supported by wealthy churches like yours and mine. Most of us give out of our abundance and we rarely feel a pinch. Yet these people give out of their poverty, in the same spirit as the widow whom Christ observed giving her last small coin when she had nothing left to eat. Jesus remarked, "this poor widow has put in more than all the others."[6] Apparently God uses different accounting methods than we do.

It is not just the economically needy that we are compelled to give to, but the needy of all forms: lonely, ill, rejected, hurting. Often we don't have to go too far to find these people. But if we are sensitive to their needs they can many times be found right in our own church family.

At a recent high school camp several of the kids who attended were mentally handicapped. These kids could not join in most of the activities that the rest of the students enjoyed. They could not even carry on much of a conversation that would be of interest to the average person. Besides they looked and acted a little awkward and therefore most of the campers, while polite, made little detours around them whenever possible. Yet these handicapped students were aware of the need to enjoy the company of other human beings. They were needy.

One afternoon as I was working on a project in the kitchen area I noticed one of the handicapped girls come into the dining hall. She stared out the window and tapped her feet to the music being played there.

Kids came in and out of the dining room for the next few minutes as I worked on my little project. One of those kids was Calvin, a big, strong sixteen-year-old. Calvin saw the young handicapped girl staring out of the window and approached.

"How are you doing?" he asked, initiating the conversation. "Fine," the girl replied, obviously surprised that someone was talking to her. "Are you enjoying camp?" Calvin asked. "Oh yes, very much," the girl slurred. "What do you like best?" Calvin questioned.

And so for several minutes a young man with nothing to gain and even a bit to risk (such as "so you have a new girl friend" jokes from some of the more callous campers) spent his time giving to one who needed human attention and who had little ability to pay back.

I have a strong suspicion that all the great spiritual

things that occurred at the camp, the messages, the sharing, the commitments and the rest, the thing that will be first on the list in heaven will be a few minutes of conversation between a big high school kid and a mentally handicapped girl.

Perhaps there is irony in the fact that in the process of giving to the needy we get rich. We don't get rich in the things that matter to most people in this world. We gain in the things that really matter in the real Church of Jesus: love, a conscience at peace, fellowship with our neighbors, and a pleased Father in heaven.

But to be a giving Church costs us something. We must sacrifice. We must let go of our grip on the things that we cannot really keep anyhow and live contrary to the wisdom of this world. It is hard to do, but we have a good Teacher. He knows how to give. He gave us an example to follow—on Calvary.

DISCUSSION QUESTIONS

Thinking of the people you encounter in daily life, who can you identify as the "least of these"? What are some of their needs? To which of these needs can you minister?

What do you see as the limitations on your ability to help others? Which of these limitations are beyond your control to change? Which ones *can* you change? How?

What may happen as a result of your response to someone's need? How do you think the reaction of

others to your giving will affect your willingness to give again?

Read Matthew 25:40. What does this describe as a Christian's motivation for helping others?

NOTES
1. Mark 12:31
2. 1 Timothy 5:9-16
3. Acts 20:33-35
4. James 1:27
5. Matthew 25:35-40
6. Luke 21:3

ELEVEN

GOD HAS NO FAVORITES — THE CHURCH SHOULDN'T EITHER

Christ Jesus came into the world to save sinners—of whom I am the worst. But for that very reason I was shown mercy . . . as an example for those who would believe on him and receive eternal life. 1 Timothy 1:15,16

Do nothing out of selfish ambition or vain conceit, but in humility consider others better than yourselves. Each of you should look not only to your own interests, but also to the interests of others.
Philippians 2:3,4

I live in Hawaii and I travel a great deal. As soon as someone learns where I am from it is a sure bet that they will need to make a comment. Oftentimes I hear "Suffering for Jesus, huh?" to which I reply, "It's a tough job, but someone has to do it!" On other occasions people will tell about the times they visited the islands or they will ask if I know "so and so." ("So and so" usually lives hundreds of miles away on another island.)

It was no big surprise when I got a similar reaction from Tony Campolo. (I mentioned my home during a late night dinner.) For those of you who do not know Tony, just imagine a man who looks like a small Italian version of Don Rickles and who has so much energy that it seems he must have been lacing his coffee with jet fuel. Then throw in a streak of brilliance and big hunk of intensity, flair for boldness, and a talent for speaking. There you have him. Tony is a popular speaker around the country.

Recently our separate ministries brought Tony and me to the same town. The organization sponsoring Tony's speaking engagement asked me to take him out to dinner. The hour was late and as is my habit when driving in a strange city, I became lost.

After winding through a maze of unfamiliar streets we finally found a cafe that looked promising. By the time our food arrived we were involved in conversation. "I had an interesting thing happen in Honolulu," Tony said in between bites of baked bread. What followed was one of the most fascinating stories I had ever heard.

Tony arrived in Honolulu late one night. Since he had flown several thousand miles his body clock was six hours ahead of Honolulu time. It was 1:00 A.M. but Tony's body was telling him to get up and go to work. It made sleep impossible.

Honolulu is a twenty-four hour city. People come and go at all hours of the night and there are innumerable cafes that bustle with business every hour of the day.

Tony got out of bed and put on his clothes. He wandered the balmy streets of Waikiki before finally settling on a brightly lit restaurant in which to have a cup of coffee.

As he perched on the vinyl stool at the counter Tony began to notice the other diners. They were almost exclusively women—provocatively dressed. They were just getting off work. They were prostitutes who appear at dusk each evening along Hotel Street.

Tony, an ordained minister, sat quietly on his stool listening to the conversation being bantered by these ladies of the night. Most of them talked shop about the weird "johns" they picked up that night or the trouble that some "sister" was having with her "old man."

One woman, larger and older than most of the women, was talking about her birthday. Tony caught her name—Agnes.

"I'm going to be forty-three tomorrow," announced Agnes. (This is getting towards the end of the road for someone in her profession.) The women sitting with her immediately spurted out, "Well then, happy birthday!"

"You wanna know something?" Agnes said in a voice that carried a trace of sorrow, "I never had a birthday party in my whole life."

The other women asked in stunned disbelief, "Never? How about as a kid? Surely every kid has had a birthday party."

"Never!" declared Agnes.

This little revelation said a great deal to Tony as he sat on his cafe stool. No birthday party probably means that Agnes was raised in a home where she didn't get the kind of love and care that kids deserve. Her occupation as a prostitute seemed to be a little more understandable in this light. Agnes was a hurting human being underneath the made-up, high-gloss exterior.

Tony signaled the restaurant manager and asked quietly, "Do these girls come in here every night?"

"Like clockwork at about this time," replied the manager.

"Agnes too?" asked Tony.

"Agnes always," shot back the manager.

"Listen," Tony continued, "if I give you the money would you arrange a surprise birthday party for Agnes tomorrow night?"

The manager stared in shock for a few moments and then nodded in agreement. Tony introduced himself and pulled out cash and handed it to the cafe manager.

The following evening after Tony had spoken to a gathering of Christians, he went back to his hotel. At 2:30 A.M. he walked down Hotel Street to the all night cafe. As he walked into the restaurant he smiled to see balloons and streamers draped across the walls and lighting fixtures. On the counter sat a large birthday cake which spelled out "Happy Birthday Agnes" in thick pink icing.

The cafe was loaded with prostitutes. Apparently someone had done a great job of getting the word out about the surprise party.

Tony took his place on a stool and waited for Agnes to arrive.

Before long Agnes pushed through the door of the restaurant and before she had a chance to notice the bright decorations all of the patrons were on their feet cheering "Happy Birthday!"

Agnes was taken back. "For *me*?" she asked in shock. "I, I've never had a birthday party before."

Someone presented Agnes with the cake. Huge tears welled in her makeup-covered eyes. She stared at her cake and sobbed, "For me? For me?"

Finally Tony said, "OK Agnes, let's cut the cake."

"What?" cried Agnes.

"Let's cut the cake," said Tony. "We all want something to eat."

Horror flashed across Agnes's face. "It's my cake," she said. "I've never had a birthday cake." Agnes picked up the cake and sheltered it with her arms. "I've never had a cake before. It's my cake. You can't just *cut* it," she sobbed. Huge tears rolled down her cheeks. Then Agnes

132 THE CHURCH

still sobbing and clutching her cake ran out of the restaurant.

The onlookers were touched. The manager leaned over the counter and broke the silence by asking Tony, "Hey mister, just what kind of church are you the preacher of anyways?"

Tony looked at the manager and replied, "The kind of church that gives birthday parties for hookers."

Tony was exactly right. The real Church *is* the kind of church that gives birthday parties for hookers. We have our example in Jesus himself.

Jesus was often accused of hanging out with the wrong people. His disciples were crude fishermen, tax collectors, and nobodies from the "sticks." His dinner companions were often traitors to the Jewish cause, drunkards, and even prostitutes.

Jesus claimed that He associated with these people because they were obviously the ones who knew they needed Him. "It is not the healthy who need a doctor, but the sick," He said.[1]

Jesus recognized the humanity and potential of the people society had written off. His compassion was all that was needed to revive their humanity and their dignity and to reclaim their wasted lives.

As we walk with Jesus, His way of seeing the potential in people can rub off on us. We can see the possibilities for greatness in those who have been cast off. We can show his compassion to a hurting world.

Tony saw in Agnes a person who still had worth. Someone, in whom a flicker of hope still could be seen through the eyes of Jesus. Perhaps her life could be drawn to Jesus by the selfless kindness of one of His people. G.K. Chesterton once wrote, "There is a great man who makes every man feel small. But the real great man is the man who makes every man feel great."[2]

One of the duties of the Church is to make every person we touch feel that they have worth, value, and significance. We are to encourage the weak to become great men and women, to treat each other as special and worthy. It is our duty to express this attitude to every age group and across every racial, economic, educational, and political barrier.

The idea that each person has great value sets Christianity apart from many other philosophies of the world. Philosophies such as communism, nationalism, and fascism hold that the good of the nation, state, or tribe is of greater importance than the good of its individuals. The nation after all, will continue serving the common good of the majority long after its individual members die. When individuals die they are gone. But the state lives on, they reason.

But, if, as Christians believe, the individual lives on forever, then the whole life span of the greatest empire is but a blink of time in eternity. In this case, the individual is vastly more important than the survival of any political system or government.

Couple eternal destiny with the facts that all people are made in the image of God[3] and God desires all people to be reconciled to Him[4] and you have a powerful foundation for understanding why Christians believe human life is sacred. Because human life is sacred Christians are concerned about issues such as abortion. Christians hold that the life of the unborn child is of far greater importance than the inconvenience the pregnancy might be to the woman bearing the child or to her parents, the father, taxpayers, or anyone else called upon to share the burden.

Christianity swarms with ideas of this sort. Jesus often told His followers that they should invest in things of eternal value.[5] One eternal investment is treating others in a manner that makes them feel they have worth. In fact, Jesus promised that the people who did this would be rewarded—but not in worldly currency.[6]

This kind of thinking-about-the-other-fellow idea is first of all the responsibility of individuals. What you do about the "out of it" kid you walk by every day at school is your responsibility. It is solely up to you, as a member of Christ's Church to make sure that kid knows you see some great things in him. It is your job to let the overweight girl or the guy with terrible acne know they are not a modern day leper because they don't fit the pretty image pushed by TV and magazines. You will become great in your school not because you make others look silly, uncool, or insignificant, but because you make them feel like they are great.[7]

But determining to put the other guy first is not only an individual decision it is also a group decision. Let me give you an example.

Although it is a common practice, it has always struck me as odd for churches to ask certain people to be "greeters" on Sunday morning. In case you don't know, a greeter is a person who has been assigned the job of being nice to new people visiting the church. They usually are equipped with an "How are ya" smile and a handful of brochures about the activities of the church. Another part of their job is to get the names and addresses of visitors so that someone else in the church (usually from the Visitation Committee) can go and visit the new people. Many times greeters can be found at the exit doors of a church, wearing a name tag that says "greeter" and eyeballing the crowd for an unfamiliar face to tackle.

What strikes me as being so bizarre about this is that it seems obvious from Scripture that greeting new people and making an attempt to get to know them should be a natural part of what all Christians do, not a job assigned to a few. It seems a sad joke that so many Christians have not grasped this concept despite their many hours in the pew.

Having values that conflict with the world's point of view can be a difficult thing. We are a lot more indoctrinated to the world's standards than we think. See what your reaction might be to the following situations.

Your sister has been asked out by a strong, fairly handsome young man. According to those who know him, he is kind, gentle, and has a good sense of humor. He also quit school at seventeen and now works as a city garbage collector.

Do you encourage your sister to go out with this guy?

Do you make jokes about his job or the kind of car he is likely to drive?

Do you think your parents would care if your sister got serious about this young man?

If you are a girl, would you be interested in this kind of guy?

A guy from your sister's work wants her to go out with a friend of his. The guy has tatoos, bleached hair, and has been known to expose himself publicly on occasion. His language is almost always full of obscenities. He has a reputation for using girls. He usually throws a hostile sneer at those who look at him.

He would like to come over and pick up your sister.
Do you think she should go out with him?
Would you like to meet him?
His name is Billy Idol.

If you are like most people, you may tend to overlook the first guy's good character and view his job as a point of disqualification. On the other hand, most of us would not want our sister to go out with the second guy—unless he happens to be famous. Then we will overlook his meanness and vulgarity and call him an eccentric.

The tug to make choices based on the popularity of people, or their money, status, or fame is part of the worldly thinking that we must give up. It is not Christ's way.

As the Bible points out God does not call many people who are wise by human standards. He does not target the influential, powerful, or upper class. Rather, He chose the foolish, the lowly, and the simple in order to work in them such a transformation that they confound the wise.[8]

Most of what Jesus has to say about out treatment of others is summed up in what is called the Golden Rule: "Do to others what you would have them do to you."[9] This idea, by the way, is found stated similarly in many other religions. Clearly it is one of those concepts that God tucked into the minds and hearts of humans from the very beginning.

Now treating people as you would want to be treated does not mean that you need to become weak-willed. There is no need to let everyone off for every offense. We are not required to give everyone everything that they desire.

Most of us, for instance, expect consequences when we do wrong things. None of us would expect a teacher to give us an *A* in English if we didn't turn in our homework and flunked every test we took. We would receive a failing grade and we would know that we deserved it. In flunking us the teacher might even be doing to others what she would have them do to her, since she knows that receiving a grade not earned is not good for anyone. The fair grade is better in the long run even if it makes us mad for the time.

Most of us as children would have liked to eat candy all day and never have to brush our teeth. Our parents however took away candy and forced us to brush our teeth. At the time this upset many of us. In our childish lack of wisdom we might even have said that our parents were violating the Golden Rule. After maturing with our teeth and health intact we can look back and agree with what our parents did. They treated us just as they would want to be treated if they were the children and we the parents.

The Golden Rule pushes us to consider what's best for others. It does not allow us to write off people. It will not allow us the luxury of our own private, self-indulgent world. It forces us out into a world where we can make a difference. When practiced by a group of believers, it makes a church attractive, warm, caring, and loving— even to prostitutes who have never had a birthday party.

DISCUSSION QUESTIONS

When meeting someone for the first time, what characteristics of that person would make a positive impression on you? What characteristics

would make a negative impression? How would these impressions affect your attitude toward that person?

What can you say or do to express to someone else that they have value?

How can your youth group show concern for people whom you as an individual would have a hard time reaching?

NOTES
1. Matthew 9:12
2. G.K. Chesterton, *Charles Dickens, The Last of the Great Men*, (New York: The Readers Club, 1947), p. 8.
3. Genesis 1:27
4. 1 Timothy 2:4
5. Matthew 6:19-21
6. Luke 6:35,36
7. Matthew 23:11-12
8. 1 Corinthians 1:26,27
9. Matthew 7:12

TWELVE
THE HEARTBEAT OF GOD

I urge, then, first of all, that requests, prayers, intercession and thanksgiving be made for everyone—for kings and all those in authority, that we may live peaceful and quiet lives in all godliness and holiness.
1 Timothy 2:1,2

Where two or three come together in my name, there am I with them.
Matthew 18:20

All of us have seen marching bands. Most high schools and colleges have them hiking around during football games. They are a common sight at parades. One thing that all marching bands have in common is that they march in step. Band members must not only remember the music they are playing, but also the cadence they are marching to.

Even the most superb musician will look like a fool if he is out of step. Band members who march to a different beat run the risk of arriving before the rest of the band, falling behind, or crashing into another musician.

It would be a highly unusual marching band that allowed its members to do anything they wanted to do when they wanted to do it. If there is such a band, its practices must be chaotic and I doubt that many committees invite it to participate in parades.

The Church is like a marching band. It is a group of individuals trying to walk to the same beat.

If it is hard for you to picture the Church as a marching band, try to see it as a rock group.

Most of us have been to concerts. We've seen our favorite musicians tearing into their music. In some specific ways the Church is very much like a band of rock 'n' roll musicians.

In a rock group, each musician is uniquely talented. Some have a sense of rhythm. Others may have an ability to play a tune, sing a song, or write words to sing. Each individual must synchronize his talents with the others. The drummer, bassist, rhythm guitarist, and lead guitarist all have their appointed parts. The idea is for the whole band to work together in such a way that they end up with a pleasurable sound called music. The effect of the band members working together is greater than the effect of them working independently (something called synergism). Done the right way, music is good in itself and attractive to others.

In order for a band to produce music that people enjoy, musicians must accomplish certain things. They must become proficient in the instrument of their choice. This process usually takes much time, practice, and dedication. The musician must understand the basic principles of music.

To work together as a band, its members must also follow the melody and beat of the music. Regardless of how talented a group of musicians are, they won't produce music if each one plays his own song at the same time other members are playing theirs. Any band member deciding to do his own thing with the beat won't last long in a group.

142 THE CHURCH

In the Christian life it is Jesus who sets the beat or cadence for us to follow. That beat pulses through the words of Scripture and through the Holy Spirit that dwells within us. It vibrates through everything God has created and through the halls of eternity. It is the meter of God Himself, His heartbeat.

It is up to each of us to keep in step with that heavenly beat. This often does not come easily, especially to those who have spent a long time out of step and out of tune with God's will.

Like musicians, each of us must learn to develop the skills we have been given by God, both the spiritual gifts the Bible says we have and our inborn talents.[1] We must practice those things just as we must work to develop a skill in art, communication, or interpersonal relations. Then we must put these gifts and talents to use for God.

In a band the better its members play in tune with each other the better the sound will be. In a church the more people keep in step with God the sweeter and more inviting the church will be. The opposite is also true. If the people who make up a church are out of sync with God, it will become evident. The church will lack His sweet spirit. Such churches seldom grow.

It is important to remember that keeping in step with the heartbeat of God is a continuous effort. Just like struggling musicians, Christians may sometimes hit sour notes in their spiritual music and at other times their walk may step exactly to God's rhythm. It is the long stretch of keeping a Christlike cadence that makes the difference.

The spiritual synchronization of the Church starts with us—with our private and personal devotional lives. The more disciplined we are at practicing it, the better the results will be.

Imagine a group of people who were only fed once or twice a week. Imagine that they were expected to go out from their feedings to do things of great importance, to win battles, climb mountains, or struggle with foes. It is doubtful that any of these undernourished people could be counted on to do much more than to stumble back to the dining hall each week for another meal. They would be ineffective because of lack of good food.

Much of the true Church suffers from spiritual malnutrition. Many Christians have enough physical food each week but are lacking the important spiritual vitamins needed in order to live the Christian life as it should be lived. It is not because there is a lack of spiritual nourishment available. It is because many in the Church do not take the time they should to feed themselves on God's Word, to spend time talking to Him, hearing His heartbeat and walking to its rhythms. Instead, many depend on pre-digested weekly meals in church services to give them the strength they need to live the Christian life. It is rarely enough.

For years Christians have referred to a time of privately listening to God's heartbeat as their "devotional life." It has become very popular to recommend that people get involved in some sort of a program to insure that they have an allotted time to make contact with God. These programs may consist of specific Bible readings to follow, devotional books to meditate upon, prayer lists to help facilitate long and more meaningful prayer times, and often a prescribed time of day during which they can focus on their spiritual development.

Often people who cannot live up to the discipline of a particular devotional program find themselves discouraged and feeling guilty. They feel as though they have let God down. All this guilt and discouragement may cause some Christians to give up their efforts. This is sad because although Jesus modeled prayer and encouraged His followers to pray, no specific formula for a person's devotional life is given in Scripture. The formulas are inventions of well-meaning Christians.

In order to have a truly meaningful devotional life, each Christian should try to understand what prayer really is and then develop a devotional discipline that fits his or her own life-style.

Whatever system is used by people in private devotions, several elements are almost always present. One is either Bible reading, or thinking and reflecting on either a particular Bible passage or on an attribute of God. The other thing that is almost always present is communicating with God in prayer.

For many Christians in the infancy of their faith, prayer is merely talking to God in the same fashion as children talk to the department store Santa at Christmastime. They present their requests and try to be good boys and girls so that "Santa God" will deliver.

Fortunately as we mature spiritually God becomes bigger to us. He does not actually grow, but our growth allows us to see His greater grandeur.

Often people in the Church will talk eagerly about prayer as if it is the same as having a conversation with another human. But as anyone who prays often will tell you, having a personal relationship with God is different from having a personal relationship with a man or woman.

God has seldom spoken audibly to anyone who has prayed to Him. He is spirit and the little nuances of human conversation are missing: body language, eye contact, physical presence. God's physical arms are not there for support nor do we see Him nod in affirmation at our requests.

Praying to God is a unique experience. It is mystical and quiet yet as sure, real, and powerful as gravity. The point of contact can be experienced but it is not easy to describe. God speaks to us as God speaks; we speak to Him as humans.

Both prayer and worship have a great deal more to do with our personal desire for God and our moment-by-moment surrender to His wisdom than they do with following a program for home devotions or the order of service for a Sunday meeting.

For example, the Bible tells believers to pray without ceasing.[2] Logically this cannot mean that we are to spend every moment of the day on our knees with eyes closed. To understand this command we must clarify our concept of prayer.

Prayer is not so much an activity but a state of mind. For Christians it is an attitude of awareness of God's presence—like being in a house with another person, each involved in independent activities yet still aware of the other person's presence.

Perhaps this idea can be demonstrated best by a comparison. Have you ever been driving in a car when a catchy song comes on the radio? It has a familiar beat, you tap your fingers in rhythm, the refrain is easy to remember and sticks in your mind long after the car has pulled into the driveway and stopped. You find yourself sitting in your room tapping your fingers and humming the song hours after you heard it. This is like prayer—humming the tune God has sung all day long. Going about the daily things of life with the heavenly beat in the background of our minds, ready to break out at a moment's notice.

146 THE CHURCH

Of course many of the other things people often teach about prayer are true as well. It is praise, petition, and confession. But these things are elements of prayer and not the thing itself.

It's a similar way worshiping God is not only a part of a church service but is also the day-to-day letting go of our own silly and self-serving rule and clinging to God. The things that take place in a worship service—singing, praying, listening to a sermon—are elements of worship. They are not the thing itself. People who only go to church for a spiritual recharge usually struggle in everyday living. They have not learned the secret of moment-by-moment surrender of their minds and wills to God.

This is not to say that Christians have no need to get together. We do. The Bible states "Let us not give up meeting together . . . but let us encourage one another,"[3] "Love the brotherhood of believers,"[4] and "God's household . . . is the church of the living God, the pillar and foundation of the truth."[5] These verses show how important the fellowship of believers is.

When Christians gather together, in most cases once or twice a week, the Bible says that a powerful, almost mystical thing occurs: Jesus is there, present with the believers.[6] At times it may seem that God is not present. This is caused by our allowing things to compete for our attention or to block our experiencing His presence. God is just as much there as He is when our senses respond to even the most subtle evidences of His presence. This fact alone should make our time together as believers uniquely special.

But often it isn't special at all. Sometimes it is, well, just plain boring. This in part may be because some worship services contain things that may seem to have little to do with our everyday walk with God.

Although many of the traditions practiced in church do have significance and deep meaning, those meanings may not be explained to members of the church in a way they understand. This makes it hard for some people to get to the heart of the service.

For example, many churches practice a thing called "responsive reading" (also called a "litany"). The idea behind this is to involve the congregation in talking to God through the use of a written prayer. First the pastor speaks his lines and then the congregation reads their part from a prayer book or a hymnal. Sometimes the responsive reading is a psalm. Other times it may be a newly written prayer. But the experience can be boring if you don't understand the purpose of the practice. But if a person knows that it is a form of united prayer the experience is enhanced.

In the same way the idea behind the pastor leading a group in prayer is not so that you can nod off while the pastor is busy talking to God. It is an effort to have the whole congregation join with the minister in spirit and acknowledge his words as being what they feel, too. The "amen" at the end of a prayer is a way the congregation can say, "I agree."

Even singing hymns involves more than it may seem. Hymns are not just an effort to make pretty music or to drown out the person next to you with your own voice. They are supposed to be words sung to God or about Him.

Understanding some of the practices of your church can help you participate in it. When you participate you have a hard time getting bored.

Obviously some of the things that occur in church meetings are truly boring or just don't work. Sometimes a speaker talks way beyond his listeners' attention spans. The great apostle Paul even "talked on and on" so long on one occasion that one of his listeners drifted off to sleep and fell off the third story window ledge where he had been sitting.[7] Sometimes a sermon topic deals with a subject that is too difficult or too ethereal to grasp.

When we feel that the service is boring, too long, or difficult to understand we may be tempted to gripe and complain about how dry church is. But before we do that we must take into account the possibility that there may be those who have much longer attention spans than we do or who have a much larger vocabulary, or who deal with many more abstract thoughts. These people will probably think that the worship service was great!

But if a person often has problems with being bored in church there are things that he can do besides stop going. He can contact the pastor and ask why the church does certain things—discover the meaning behind some of the ritual. A person can suggest alternatives. Many pastors are very open to a young person who says honestly, "I really want to enjoy the worship service but I have a real hard time concentrating. Perhaps we could figure out a way that younger or less experienced Christians can get more out of the time."

Young people can ask their parents or other adults to speak to the church staff on their behalf. Some pastors will be more receptive to this approach.

It is important to note that whenever going to someone to complain about a particular service or activity it is a good idea to offer some alternatives that might actually work. Be specific about what you don't understand or enjoy. Be willing to bend and give. If the church is made up of various kinds and ages of people, realize that the church leadership will have a difficult time pleasing everyone all the time.

If nothing else, worship can be an enjoyable time for you and God to get on a little more familiar terms. Use the time to read your Bible, jot down questions raised by Scripture or the sermon, or pray.

Because churches are made of people, they can be very different and often very imperfect. There is no such thing as a perfect church because there are no perfect people. But some fellowships seem to do a better job than others.

Sometimes it becomes necessary for a person to change fellowships in order that he can better develop his spiritual life or better use his abilities. This is a step that should only be taken after much prayer and consideration.

The church we gather with is a reflection of its people. If we are warm, friendly, and forgiving, very likely the church will be that way too. If we genuinely love God and try to serve Him, our example will be infectious. We are the Church. Its stand or its compromise in this world depends largely upon us. We are the tools that God has chosen to use to show His image to the world. We can shake the earth—or we can quiver with it.

DISCUSSION QUESTIONS

Describe your personal relationship with God. When do your thoughts turn towards God? What activities and attitudes help you be more aware of God's presence?

What time of day are you least preoccupied and

most able to focus on God? How can you use that time to develop a deeper, more meaningful relationship with Him?

What aspects of your church's worship service are the most meaningful to you? Why? What aspects are the most confusing or meaningless? What can you do to get more meaning out of the worship service?

NOTES
1. 1 Corinthians 12:7-11
2. 1 Thessalonians 5:17
3. Hebrews 10:25
4. 1 Peter 2:17
5. 1 Timothy 3:15
6. Matthew 18:20
7. Acts 20:7-12